Rig

the Word of Truth
Scripture, Canon, and Creed

CONTRIBUTORS

Carl E. Braaten
Robert Benne
Stephen J. Hultgren
David S. Yeago
Mark A. Grandquist
Amy C. Shifrin, STS
Christopher R. Seitz

Edited by
Carl E. Braaten

Lectures Presented
at a Theological Conference
Sponsored by Lutheran CORE
and the
North American Lutheran Church

Charleston, South Carolina
July 22-23, 2014

ALPB Books
Delhi, New York

For a **FREE COPY** of
Lutheran Forum and *Forum Letter*
go online at: www.lutheranforum.org
and click on "Free Issue"

Cover photo:
General Pelot Summerall Chapel at the Citadel
in Charleston, South Carolina,
taken by Frederick J. Schumacher

The American Lutheran Publicity Bureau wishes
to acknowledge with deep appreciation the work of
William Fensterer for the proofreading of this text,
Frederick J. Schumacher for acting as project manager,
and Martin A. Christiansen for layout and design work.

Paul Robert Sauer
Executive Director, ALPB

ISBN 1-892921-29-4

American Lutheran Publicity Bureau
PO Box 327
Delhi, NY 13753

Rightly Handling the Word of Truth: Scripture, Canon, and Creed
(Delhi, NY: ALPB Books, 2014), 129 pp.

Contents

Presenters

Dr. Robert Benne
Jordan-Trexler Professor of Religion Emeritus,
Founder and Director of the Center for Religion
and Society at Roanoke College, Salem, Virginia

Rev. Dr. Carl E. Braaten
Professor Emeritus of Systematic Theology
at the Lutheran School of Theology at Chicago
Sun City West, Arizona

Rev. Dr. Mark A. Granquist
Associate Professor of Church History
Luther Seminary, St. Paul, Minnesota

Rev. Dr. Stephen J. Hultgren
Lecturer in New Testament, Australian Lutheran College
North Adelaide, South Australia, Australia

Rev. Dr. Amy C. Schifrin, STS
President of the North American Lutheran Seminary
and Associate Professor of Liturgy and Homiletics,
Trinity School for Ministry, Ambridge, Pennsylvania

Rev. Dr. Christopher R. Seitz
Senior Research Professor, Wycliffe College,
Toronto School of Theology, Toronto, Ontario, Canada

Dr. David S. Yeago
Professor of Systematic Theology and Ethics,
North American Lutheran Seminary,
Trinity School for Ministry, Ambridge, Pennsylvania

Preface

Carl E. Braaten

This is the fifth theological conference sponsored by Lutheran Coalition for Renewal and the North American Lutheran Church. It marks the passing of the baton of leadership from Benne and Braaten to Schifrin, Hinlicky, Nelson, and Yeago. As they say at AllState, you will be in good hands. There is a way for me to be present with you despite my unavoidable absence and that is to say a few valedictory words that Benne asked me to provide as a preface to his introduction of the conference.

The speakers at this conference will teach us how to read and understand the Bible aright. We all know how easy it is to get it wrong. It is not enough to believe the Bible is the Word of God. The Mormons do that and get it wrong. It is not enough to believe in the authority and inspiration of the Bible. The Jehovah Witnesses do that, and get it wrong. The big-name heretics, sectarians, and schismatics in church history believed in the authority of Scripture, even its inerrancy, and presumably got a lot of things wrong. So where's the rub? What must we do to rightly handle the Bible as the Word of God's truth? The subtitle of this conference was chosen intentionally to offer some clues – Scripture, Canon, and Creed. The concept of canon suggests that the Bible is the church's book and the concept of creed suggests that the church has a "rule of faith" to guide its interpretation of the Bible.

The four previous theological conferences have prepared the way for us to tackle the most embattled doctrine in American Christianity – the battle over the Bible. When we get that wrong, everything else goes bad in the church. That's how we got into the situation of having to found a new movement – Lutheran CORE – and a new church body – the North American Lutheran Church. Something went terribly wrong in the way Scripture was interpreted or better, misinterpreted by many bishops and theologians in the Evangelical Lutheran Church in America. And this is happening not only among Lutherans everywhere but virtually all denominations are being fractured by the same crisis.

When I began the study of theology in the early 1950s, a huge controversy was raging whether to use or reject the modern methods of historical criticism to interpret the Bible. Failure to resolve the issue has led to schisms, most notably the 1970's schism in the Missouri Synod. The bleeding has not stopped. Whereas the use of the modern critical methods are here to stay – no church will be able to turn back the clock – they cannot flourish in the church and theology as a free-floating preoccupation of academics out of touch with the living tradition of the church. The "Jesus Seminar" is now history, but it offered proof positive of how biblical research runs amok when canon and creed are ignored and even despised.

Our previous theological conferences have made clear that the authority and interpretation of the Bible rest on two essential pre-conditions. The one is ecclesial – the place of the church in using the Bible as the normative resource to define its identity and mission, its being and doing, as the community calling itself Christian. Where there is no church there is no Bible and no need for it. We do believe that the Holy Spirit is the supreme author of Holy Scripture by moving human authors to put in writing the message of salvation and we believe with equal conviction that the same Spirit continues to guide the church to interpret these inspired writings. Neither the gates of hell nor any errant church bureaucracy or assembly can prevail against what the Holy Spirit has in store for the universal church of Christ.

The second pre-condition of rightly dividing the word of truth is centered in the confession of Christ as the "way, the truth, and the life." The final revelation of the God of the Bible is centered in Christ, the one and only hope of salvation. The new things the Bible announces are centered in Christ. For the church and all Christians the ultimate authority of the Bible depends on its witness to Jesus Christ.

While some of my friends, in trying to escape the cultural captivity of American Lutheranism, went wandering off into other denominations, what kept me tethered to the Lutheran tradition was Luther's Christ-centered interpretation of the Bible, his famous dictum: "This is the true test of all books, when we see whether or not they preach Christ. For all the Scriptures show us Christ (Rom. 3: 21) and St. Paul will know nothing but Christ (I Cor. 2: 2). Whatever does not teach Christ is certainly not apostolic, even though St. Peter or St. Paul teaches it. Again whatever preaches Christ would be apostolic, even though Judas, Ananias, Pilate or Herod were doing it." We get the point.

In planning this conference we were guided by the hope that these two pre-conditions of biblical authority and interpretation – the churchly context and the Christic content – will come to forceful expression so that we will learn to love the Bible more and renew our trust in the words of Scripture because of our love for its Lord.

Introduction

Robert Benne

Welcome to you all on Carl Braaten's and my behalf. It has been truly inspiring to get up here for five successive years and see hundreds of people gathered at their own expense to hear theological lectures. We thank you profusely for your support, as we thank all the persons who have worked behind the scenes to make these conferences go.

We have picked quite a lively topic for this conference: Rightly Handling the Word of Truth ... or, in other words, the right interpretation of the Bible. The mainline Protestant churches are all in various stages of division over this very topic. Can the Bible be interpreted to turn the Great Commission into inter-religious dialog? Can the Bible be interpreted in such a way as to exchange repentance, justification, and the call to obedience for the gospel of radical inclusion? Can the Bible be made to support gay marriage? Can the Bible be interpreted to portray Jesus as a peasant revolutionary, a cynic philosopher, a model of theocentric piety, or a teacher of non-violence? What is central and essential to biblical truth and what can be bargained away to accommodate the cultural and intellectual challenges of the day?

There have been many answers to the challenge of how to rightly interpret the Bible. One familiar answer in American history is that everyone has just as much access to the truth as anyone else. Some have believed that the "priesthood of all believers" means just that. One prominent nineteenth century Lutheran I have been studying lately – Samuel

Simon Schmucker (the mentor of the great founder of Roanoke College, David Bittle) – believed that anyone with good common sense could interpret the Bible rightly. In his reading key distinctive Lutheran doctrines – the Real Presence, baptismal regeneration, the two-kingdoms doctrine – were unbiblical and therefore had to be discarded. I was shocked to find out that his motto was *sola scriptura!*

Well, if it's not Scripture alone, how about adding the Lutheran Confessions (the *Book of Concord*) as the right way to interpret the Bible. But the Missouri Lutherans who left the Synod in the mid-70s thought they were better confessionalists than those who stayed. The ELCA believes it is properly confessional. But so does the NALC, and they disagree on many crucial items.

This Lutheran disarray has convinced many of our Lutheran brothers and sisters to swim the Tiber for a magisterium that can authoritatively interpret the Bible. The list of names who have followed this path is pretty long and impressive.

So, we are looking to speakers at our conference to enlighten us on these matters, though it would be naïve to expect definitive answers. But I believe we will make real progress. We have a veritable feast of topics, beginning with this evening's lecture by Stephen Hultgren. We move on tomorrow morning to David Yeago's lecture on Luther's Way of Reading and Interpreting the Bible, then on to Mark Granquist's historical account of Scripture controversies in American Lutheranism. Then we will hear from Amy Schifrin on knowing the Bible through worship and liturgy. We conclude with Christopher Seitz on the Bible and sexual ethics. I must say that I insisted on including this topic because biblical sexual ethics is under severe attack in our society and even in the churches. One other sharp attack is on the uniqueness and necessity of Christ for salvation, but we have already had a conference on that theme.

On Being "Lovers of Truth"

The Canon of Scripture and the Church's Commitment to Truth

Stephen J. Hultgren

In 2008, as debate was raging in the Evangelical Lutheran Church of America (ELCA) over issues relating to human sexuality, a retired ELCA pastor wrote a column for *The Lutheran* in which he argued that it is a kind of "selective fundamentalism" to believe that the lifelong marriage of one man and one woman is the biblical norm.[1] His reasoning? Abraham, Jacob, and David did not adhere to such a view of marriage. So how can one say that there is one biblical norm for marriage?

A Lutheran pastor ought to know better. The argument that there is no biblical norm for marriage, because Abraham was a polygamist, is rather like saying that there is no biblical view on incest, since Lot had sexual intercourse with his daughters. Only an unreflective reader of Scripture believes that any particular example of behavior in the Bible, taken out of its total canonical context, can be regarded as normative for the Christian. I begin with this case in order to illustrate the problem to be treated here, namely, what it means for the right handling of the Word of God that we have a *canon* of Scripture. It seems that in many corners of the church today canon consciousness no longer exists. Scripture is regarded as a loose collection of writings that have no particu-

---

1. Andrew E. Carlsson, "Authority & Power: They're Often Confused," *The Lutheran* (October, 2008): 53.

lar internal coherence or order. Thus, rather than seeing Jesus' teaching on the lifelong marriage of one man and one woman for what it is, namely, a clarification of God's original creative will as revealed in Genesis, forever revalidated by Jesus after humanity's fall into sin and the giving of the Mosaic law (Mark 10:2–9), and rather than taking Genesis and Jesus' teaching together as the overarching, canonical framework within which all other possible permutations of marriage or sexual relationships are to be critically evaluated – rather than this, one regards Abraham's polygamous marriage as a model for behavior equal in authority to Jesus' teaching. Jesus and the apostles are no longer accorded any privilege in teaching God's intention and will for marriage and sexuality in a final and decisive way.[2] The result of the eclipse of canon consciousness is that the church loses all rhyme and reason in the way that it develops normative teaching on the basis of Scripture.

The thesis of this paper is that rightly handling the word of truth (2 Tim 2:15) entails putting the gospel in right relationship to the whole of the received prophetic and apostolic witness of Scripture. More generally, to respect the canon of Scripture means that we will rightly relate the various parts of Scripture to each other. When we do so, we can be confident that the canon of Scripture will guide us rightly in all matters of faith, doctrine, and morals. To unfold the thesis,

---

2. One finds a similar argument even among ELCA theologians. Cf. recently Frederick J. Gaiser, "For the Nations, through the Nathans: When Word Speaks to World," *Word & World* 33/3 (2013): 211–26, here 218: "Despite the rest of the Bible's interesting diversity about the nature of marriage – you will search in vain, for example, for the supposed biblical definition of marriage as between one man and one woman – despite this, Jesus, at least, was pretty clear about divorce. We think and act differently. Why? Is it mere cultural indulgence, or have different definitions of marriage and divorce required a different response?" A full response is not possible here. I simply ask: *Should* we think and act differently? Who has defined marriage and divorce differently, why, and why is a different response from the church necessary? These questions will continue to haunt the church as long as she pledges fidelity to Holy Scripture.

we will begin with an exegesis of 2 Tim 2:15. Then we will consider what I would like to call the *problem* of the canon, the *primacy* of the canon, and the *promise* of the canon.

Exegesis of 2 Timothy 2:15

The admonition to Timothy to strive to be one who "rightly handles the word of truth" (*orthotomounta ton logon tēs alētheias*) (2 Tim 2:15) has a prominent place in the Lutheran Confessions, where the verb *orthotomein* is interpreted in the sense of "rightly distinguishing" or "rightly dividing" law and gospel.[3] The Confessions' appeal to the verse indicates that it is important for a Lutheran approach to Scripture. We shall return to Luther and the Confessions, but we begin with some considerations of the meaning of the verse within the context of the Pastoral Epistles themselves.

The so-called Pastoral Epistles, whether written by the apostle Paul himself or, as I think more likely, by someone who understood himself to be preserving and expounding the Pauline tradition in Paul's name for a later generation, are concerned to shape the doctrine, worship, ethics, and leadership in congregations that the apostle left behind. As heirs to the Pauline heritage and as recipients of the apostle's instructions, Timothy and Titus both establish a link to and stand ideally for all those who would come to exercise oversight and leadership of churches in succession to the apostle, in-

---

3. The interpretation is based on the presumed etymology of the verb, in the sense of *orthōs temnein*, "to divide rightly," which then takes on the further sense of rightly "distributing" the Word. Luther translated the verb as "recht teile." For the Confessions, see Ap. 4.188, where the sense of the Latin ("et haec [law and promise/gospel] *oportet* orthotomein, *ut ait Paulus. Videndum est, quid legi, quid promissionibus scriptura tribuat*") is explained by the German: "Denn man muß (wie Paulus sagt) recht schneiden und teilen Gottes Wort, das Gesetz auf einen Ort, die Zusage Gottes auf den andern." See also FC Ep. 5.2 and FC SD 5.1 ("recht geteilet; recte secari"). The Vulgate translates *recte tractantem verbum veritatis*. On the original meaning of the word, see below.

cluding those of us who are ordained ministers today. Let us look briefly at each of the words in the phrase *orthotomounta ton logon tes alētheias*.

In the Pastoral Epistles the "word" (*logos*) or the "word of God" ([*ho*] *logos* [*tou*] *theou*) can (apparently) refer to the (Old Testament) Scriptures (1 Tim 4:5),[4] but more often it refers to the apostolic preaching, that is, the gospel (2 Tim 2:9; 4:2; Titus 1:3; 2:5). In both the singular (1 Tim 4:12; Titus 2:8) and the plural (2 Tim 4:15) "word(s)" (*logos*/*logoi*) also refers to the "speech" of the minister, that is, preaching and teaching.[5] The speech (*logos*) or words (*logoi*) of the minister are to be normed by the deposit of faith and teaching already received; only so will the minister's word(s) and teaching be "sound" (*hygiainein*) (2 Tim 1:13–14; Titus 1:9). The affinity between the word of God/gospel and the sound speech of the minister normed by it can be seen where *logos*/*logoi* crosses over from the speech of a particular minister to the specific words that constitute the objective content for the speech of any minister in apostolic succession (2 Tim 1:13).

The "truth" (*alētheia*) that is the objective content of the "word"[6] and that is to be rightly handled (2 Tim 2:15) is, in the first instance, "the faith" (the *fides quae*),[7] the gospel of

---

4. Though commentators are not of one mind on the interpretation of *logos theou* in 1 Tim 4:5, a reference to Scripture (Gen 1:31) seems most likely. See I. Howard Marshall, *A Critical and Exegetical Commentary on the Pastoral Epistles* (Edinburgh: T & T Clark, 1999), 546; William D. Mounce, *Pastoral Epistles* (Nashville: Thomas Nelson, 2000), 241.

5. Preaching and teaching stand close to each other. Preaching and teaching can perhaps be distinguished in the sense that sound teaching follows from the basic proclamation of the gospel in preaching (1 Tim 1:10–11).

6. The genitive in *ton logon tēs alētheias* is a genitive of content or an appositive genitive: the word that contains the truth or that consists in the truth (BDF 167). Cf. Titus 1:1–3.

7. Note the parallelism between 2 Tim 2:16, 18 ("missing the mark with respect to the truth" because of teaching "profane chatter") and 1 Tim 6:20–21 ("missing the mark with respect to the faith" because of professing "the false *gnōsis*," almost synonymous with the "profane chatter").

salvation and eternal life through faith in Christ (Titus 1:1–3; cf. 1 Tim 2:4; 4:3; Eph 1:13; Col 1:5; Jas 1:18), knowledge of which follows from repentance (2 Tim 2:25) and frees one from the snares of the devil (2 Tim 2:26). But derivatively the "truth" includes the objective content of doctrine and morals that follows from faith in the gospel (1 Tim 4:1–5; cf. 1:10–11). Thus—and this is extremely important—the gospel in the strict sense is being related to a larger body of truth in which the gospel takes shape. The "truth" is something that can be known (1 Tim 2:4; 4:3; 2 Tim 2:25; 3:7–8; Titus 1:1). It is something about which one may make objective judgments of right and wrong: one can objectively "miss the mark" with respect to the truth (2 Tim 2:18), just as one can turn aside from it (2 Tim 4:4; Titus 1:14) or be bereft of it (1 Tim 6:5).

The last point, that one can miss the mark of the truth or turn aside from it, is particularly important. The verb *orthotomein* in 2 Tim 2:15 is usually translated as "rightly handle" or "rightly explain" or the like, and (idiosyncratically) as "rightly distinguish [or divide]" in the Lutheran Confessions. On the basis of the word's previous usage, however, the verb probably means something like "to cut a straight way [for someone or something]," so that someone or something can move straight ahead, or more simply to "make [a way or something else] straight."[8] With respect to our verse, we might paraphrase *orthotomein ton logon tēs alētheias* in the sense that the

---

8. The only attested uses of the verb prior to 2 Tim 2:15 are LXX Prov 3:6; 11:5, where the verb takes the object *hodous*, and the whole phrase means "to cut straights paths." The verb appears to be based on older Greek expressions that use the image of "cutting a path" metaphorically, including in contexts of speaking (Plato, Laws 7, 810e). See BDAG 722; Helmut Köster, "*temnō*, etc." TDNT 8.111–13; James Hope Moulton and Wilbert Francis Howard, *A Grammar of New Testament Greek. Vol. II: Accidence and Word-Formation* (Edinburgh: T & T Clark, 1929), 2.274, who emphasize the first of the two verbal roots (*orthos*) of the word: "to direct, apply faithfully"; similarly Martin Dibelius and Hans Conzelmann, *The Pastoral Epistles* (tr. P. Buttolph and A. Yarbro; Philadelphia: Fortress Press, 1972), 111; Marshall, *Pastoral Epistles*, 749.

minister is to treat the "word of truth" (the gospel) in such a way that it is not twisted but rather moves straight ahead to reach its goal (bringing people to the knowledge of the truth and salvation) without hindrance or diversion.[9] The author identifies as one of the major threats to the "straight" treatment of the word of truth what he calls "profane chatter," a kind of shorthand for the false teaching that he was combating (1 Tim 4:7; 6:20; cf. Titus 1:14). This "profane chatter" is a kind of speech (*logos*!) that is not normed by the truth and that leads to greater and greater impiety (2 Tim 2:16–17). The author uses a vivid image to describe such speech, saying that it spreads like gangrene, which ruins faith and destroys its hearers, unlike the sound ("healthy") teaching that leads to salvation. The exact identity of the false teaching that the author combats is not certain, but it appears to have been either a kind of proto-gnosticism or a Judaizing Christianity or even some mix of these.[10]

The minister is to take care that his *own* words (preaching and teaching) as well as the words of others who are in his charge do not lead to confusion regarding *the* Word (the gospel) and so destroy those who hear. This care happens when the minister makes sure that his handling of the gospel

---

9. Cf. BDAG (ibid.): "guide the word of truth along a straight path (like a road that goes straight to its goal), without being turned aside by wordy debates or impious talk"; so also Marshall, *Pastoral Epistles*, 749. Köster, "*temnō*," 112, citing Gal 2:14 (*orthopodoun pros ten aletheian tou euaggeliou*), argues that the verb must relate primarily to Timothy's conduct, which is to be in accordance with the truth. The citation of Gal 2:14 is apposite, as is the observation that in Proverbs the verb is used in ethical contexts. However, in 2 Tim 2:15 *ton logon tēs aletheias* is the direct object of the verb (contrast Gal 2:14), and the context includes both conduct and teaching. Note that the verb derives from a metaphor that could be used in the context of speech in classical Greek (see previous note). Right teaching seems to be primarily in view (Marshall, *Pastoral Epistles*, 749).

10. See, e.g., Mounce, *Pastoral Epistles*, lxix–lxxxi; Marshall, *Pastoral Epistles*, 46–51; Jürgen Roloff, *Der erste Brief an Timotheus* (Zurich: Benzinger Verlag/ Neukirchen-Vluyn: Neukirchener Verlag, 1988), 228–39.

does not drive the gospel off its course of bringing about the "knowledge of the truth" on the way towards salvation. That is to say, he is to take care that speech in the church (his own and that of others in his charge) is not allowed to distract from the truth, which is the objective content of the gospel and of the doctrinal and moral teaching that follows from it.

If we ask what this care for the Word means in concrete terms, fortunately the Pastoral Epistles themselves give us some examples. I offer two examples here.

(1) In the very passage in question the author mentions two figures, Hymenaeus and Philetus, who were teaching that the resurrection had already happened (2 Tim 2:17–18), thereby "missing the mark" with respect to the truth and ruining the faith of some. We can see how this teaching is an example of steering the Word of the gospel off course. The apostle Paul taught as a matter of first importance in the gospel (1 Cor 15:1–4) that Christ was raised from the dead (15:4, 20), but he was careful to make clear that the resurrection of *believers* remains a future hope, at the return of Christ (15:22–23). Believers have not yet been raised from the dead, although they do walk in newness of life that comes from the resurrection of Christ (Rom 6:4). But already the (possibly Deutero-Pauline) epistle to the Colossians (2:12) and the (probably Deutero-Pauline) epistle to the Ephesians (2:6) teach that believers "have been raised with Christ," a way of speaking that the Paul of the unquestionably authentic letters avoids. Resurrection is used here metaphorically, but one can understand how the word might have been mistaken in a literal sense, such that "Paul" was thought to be teaching that believers had already entered the resurrection state of existence.[11] This would be a kind of overly realized eschatology, a spiritualized understanding of resurrection that left no place for a bodily resurrection and a future judgment at the *parousia*.

---

11. Compare esp. Eph 2:6 with 1:20.

We know that some gnostics held this teaching in the second century,[12] and the author of 2 Timothy may be targeting an incipient form of this teaching. The realized eschatology of the Gospel of John (e.g., 5:24; 11:23–26; cf. 8:51), read out of context, is liable to the same distortion, and it is no wonder that the Gospel of John seems to have been particularly favored by gnostics of the second century.[13]

Such a teaching is unacceptable according to the standard of apostolic tradition, because it leads or could lead to a number of problematic conclusions, such as the denial of the problem of ongoing human sinfulness, even among believers, which contradicts the gospel,[14] or a kind of fanaticism that entails an inappropriate rejection of and disengagement from the world and neglect of the gospel's own mandate to bring the world to faith, knowledge of the truth, and salvation.[15] Thus the teaching of Hymenaeus and Philetus is wrong not only because it is based on false premises about the gospel but because the teaching has further, injurious consequences for the gospel and for the larger body of apostolic teaching. The Word of the apostolic message is driven off course by false conceptions, and the result, in the words of 2 Timothy, is *katastrophē* (2:14).

---

12. See the excursus on 2 Tim 2:18 in Alfons Weiser, *Der zweite Brief an Timotheus* (Düsseldorf: Benzinger Verlag/Neukirchen-Vluyn: Neukirchener Verlag, 2003), 210–25, esp. 216–17.

13. Raymond E. Brown and Francis J. Moloney, *An Introduction to the Gospel of John* (New Haven: Yale University Press, 2003), 124–36.

14. It seems that the (proto-gnostic) opponents of the author of 1 John held to a spiritualized, overly realized eschatology that led them to claim sinlessness. See Raymond E. Brown, *The Community of the Beloved Disciple* (Mahwah: Paulist Press, 1979), 124–26; Martin Hengel, *The Johannine Question* (tr. John Bowden; London: SCM Press, 1989), 64–65. By contrast, the gospel teaches that even the justified remain liable to fall back into sin (Gal 5:17; 1 John 1:8).

15. Gnosticism had tendencies to elitism and disengagement. Cf. Kurt Rudolph, "Gnosticism," *The Anchor Bible Dictionary* (ed. David N. Freedman et al.; 6 vols.; New York: Doubleday, 1992), 2.1033–40, here 1033–34.

(2) Not unrelated to the first point, the false teaching that the author of 1 Timothy combats apparently included a false asceticism (1 Tim 4:1–5). His opponents forbade marriage and required abstention from certain foods. Once again, the author may be dealing with proto-gnostic influences.[16] In any case, one can see that the tendency towards a false asceticism is another example of a teaching that steers the Word of the gospel off course. The apostolic tradition recognized a legitimate basis for celibacy for the sake of the kingdom of God (or the gospel) as a vocational gift from God, tracing the tradition back to Jesus himself (Matt 19:10–12; 1 Cor 7:7, 25–40). But marriage was not and could not be forbidden in principle. The author of 1 Timothy does not tell us why his opponents forbade marriage, but we know that some second-century gnostics rejected marriage because it was thought to involve devotees in undesirable entanglements with the (evil) created order.[17] Such a view runs contrary to the gospel because the gospel, though teaching the fallenness of humanity and the world (Rom 3:9, 23; 5:12; 8:20, 22), upholds the goodness of marriage (1 Cor 7:28, 36). The apostolic tradition does not teach that believers can or should try to remove themselves from the created order, including marriage (1 Cor 11:11; cf. John 17:15; 1 Cor 5:10). Thus the prohibition of marriage was false, because it was based on false principles regarding the gospel. It was not drawn from the apostolic tradition but in fact stood against it.

As for the prohibition of foods, the apostolic church acknowledged a legitimate basis for abstaining from certain foods in the case of (Jewish) Christians who believed that they should still observe the Scriptural laws regarding clean

---

16. Roloff, *Der erste Brief an Timotheus*, 237.

17. Roloff, ibid. First Timothy 4:4–5 seems to be a reply primarily to the mandatory abstention from foods, and not to the prohibition of marriage, but it may also hint at the reason why the opponents rejected marriage.

and unclean foods (Rom 14:2, 14),[18] or in cases where idolatry or improper slaughter could be involved (Acts 15:20; 1 Cor 10:28). The basis in both cases was Scripture (specifically, Levitical laws). But the apostolic tradition otherwise rejected prohibitions, on the basis of the freedom of the gospel (Acts 10:1–11:18; Rom 14:14; 1 Cor 10:25–27; Gal 2:14; cf. Titus 1:15), once again tracing the believer's freedom in such matters back to Jesus (Mark 7:19).[19] In addition, Paul based freedom in matters of food on the principle that it was created by God (1 Cor 10:26), and we find a similar principle in 1 Tim 4:4–5, if, as is probable, these verses allude to Gen 1:31. Thus we see once again that the false teaching of the opponents of 1 Timothy had to be rejected because it was based on false principles that conflicted with both Scriptural principles and apostolic teaching based on the gospel.

From these examples we learn something of the highest importance for our topic. "Rightly handling the word of truth," or "making a straight way for the word of truth," is a matter of putting the gospel in right relationship to the whole of the prophetic and apostolic witness, so that the gospel is not twisted. That entails preaching and teaching the gospel in a way that honors patterns set by the Word of God in (Old Testament) Scripture, in the ministry of Jesus (as represented in apostolic tradition), and in the apostolic teaching itself.[20]

---

18. See also Matthew's (15:17) removal of the parenthetical remark in Mark 7:19.

19. I leave aside the question whether Mark 7:19 accurately interprets what the historical Jesus meant. See, e.g., E.P. Sanders, *Jewish Law from Jesus to the Mishnah: Five Studies* (London: SCM Press, 1990), 28. The removal of the parenthetical remark in Matt 15:17, seen in canonical perspective, does not so much contradict Mark as leave room for an alternative interpretation of Jesus' words that upholds the law of Moses for (Jewish) Christians who believe that they should still observe it. As Romans 14 shows, such freedom stood legitimately within the bounds of apostolic (even Pauline!) teaching.

20. According to 2 Tim 1:13 Timothy is to follow the model or pattern (*hypotyposis*) of the "sound teaching [words]" that he had heard from Paul himself.

Evangelical freedom does not permit arbitrary treatment of the prophetic and apostolic tradition. Being an apt preacher and teacher of the truth is not only a matter of proclaiming and teaching the gospel in the narrow sense; it is also a matter of drawing the right consequences of the gospel for the whole of faith, doctrine, and morals. And, finally, it is a matter of understanding the logic that underlies the shape of life and thought that the gospel takes in the world.[21]

In sum: In the Pastoral Epistles the apostolic message is in the process of becoming an objective body of true teaching in faith, doctrine, and morals, with a specific shape and specific limits. This larger body of apostolic teaching can be separated from the gospel (in the narrow sense) only at the risk of undermining the gospel itself, because when the gospel is perverted or when false consequences are drawn from it, certain foundations of the gospel itself are destroyed.[22] With these reflections on the Pastoral Epistles in mind, we come to discuss the problem of the canon.

The Problem of the Canon: Introduction

The problem that confronted the author of the Pastoral Epistles—what is the correct framework within which the gospel is to be preached and taught?—would remain a problem for the early church as it received early Christian writings, interpreted them, and made judgments as to their canonical authority. The early Christians, like people in ancient Jewish and Greco-Roman culture in general, were profoundly

---

21. For example, a person might renounce marriage either as an orthodox Christian or as a gnostic, but for vastly different reasons and with vastly different consequences.

22. For example, if I believe that as a Christian believer I have already entered resurrection existence, then I may think that I have also transcended sin and have no need of the gospel. I may also become disengaged from the world, lose my commitment to the world-wide scope of the gospel, and so undermine its purpose.

aware that written texts, once separated from their authors, were open to abuse, distortion, and misinterpretation. Already 2 Peter 3:16 names the problem for the developing Christian canon of Scripture. The Pastoral Epistles evince a beginning dependence on the written word of proto-canonical Christian writings.[23] Thus with the Pastoral Epistles we are already moving into that realm where the battle over the correct interpretation of the apostolic tradition is being joined. One can say that the Pastoral Epistles illustrate in miniature, as it were, the larger questions that the church faced in its earliest years, questions such as these: What was the proper framework within which the gospel was to be preached and taught? How did the gospel relate to the received Scriptures of Israel? How was one to distinguish between authentic and spurious witnesses to Christ in the many writings that emerged in the first two centuries of the church's life? All of these questions (and, of course, others) belong to the problem of the canon.

It is not my purpose to rehearse the history of the development of the Christian canon of Scripture. The basic outlines of that history can be found in standard works on the subject.[24] Rather, I want to focus on some of the problems that have accompanied the church's reception of the Scriptures, the way that the church has dealt with those problems, and what we might learn from them for a right handling of Scripture. We shall have to be selective. First, we shall look at Irenaeus. Secondly, we shall look at Luther and the Lutheran

---

23. The author of the Pastoral Epistles has evidently used some of Paul's writings, at least Romans and perhaps a larger collection. See Jerome D. Quinn, "Timothy and Titus, Epistles to," *The Anchor Bible Dictionary* (6 vols.; New York: Doubleday, 1992), 6.560–71, here 565. It is debated whether the author cites Luke 10:7 in 1 Tim 5:18; it seems likely to me that he does. See Roloff, *Der erste Brief an Timotheus*, 39–41; Mounce, *Pastoral Epistles*, 311; Marshall, *Pastoral Epistles*, 616–17.

24. E.g., Hans von Campenhausen, *The Formation of the Christian Bible* (tr. J.A. Baker; Philadelphia: Fortress Press, 1972).

Confessions. The goal, in both this section and the following section (on the primacy of the canon), will be to show how a right handling of the Word as we find it in the Pastoral Epistles has continued in the best of the orthodox and Lutheran heritage.

The Problem of the Canon:
Irenaeus on the Shape, the Unity, and the
Coherence of the Prophetic and Apostolic Writings

Our point of departure is Irenaeus's magnificent work *Adversus Haereses* (*Against the Heresies*), dating from the last decades of the second century. Our selection of Irenaeus as a starting point is not arbitrary. Irenaeus's unquestionable importance for the formation of the Christian canon of Scripture as well as for the proper framework for understanding the Christian Scriptures makes him an obvious place to begin.[25] But more than that, both from his frequent quotations of and allusions to the Pastoral Epistles[26] and from his concern to defend "the truth" it is clear that Irenaeus wanted to be a bishop and teacher who "rightly handles the word of truth" in the kind of faithfulness to apostolic tradition that has become familiar to us in the Pastoral Epistles.

We can gather from Irenaeus's work a number of principles for the right handling of Scripture in the church, which remain important to this day.[27] I wish to highlight three such principles.

---

25. On this see Campenhausen, *Formation*, 181–209.

26. Already the original Greek title of the work, translated as *Exposé and Overthrow of What is Falsely Called Knowledge*, alludes to 1 Tim 6:20. See further esp. Preface 1 to Book 1; 1.8.1; 1.23.4; Preface 1 to Book 2; 2.14.7; 2.21.2; 3.1.1; 4.26.4; 5.20.2. All subsequent citations in this section on Irenaeus refer to this work.

27. Eric Osborn, *Irenaeus of Lyons* (Cambridge: Cambridge University Press, 2001), 172–75, enumerates eight principles for the interpretation of Scripture in Irenaeus.

(1) For Irenaeus the prophetic and apostolic Scriptures take a specific *shape*, which is best described as an overarching narrative. The Scriptures describe one overarching story about the one God and his work in the past, present, future, with its high points in God's creation of the heavens, the earth, and humanity through his Word; humanity's fall into sin and death; the giving of the law; the sending of the prophets; the incarnation of the Word in God's Son Jesus Christ, his death, and resurrection; the sending of the apostles; the Son's return for judgment at the end of time, with the bodily resurrection of the dead and eternal life for the righteous and eternal punishment for the wicked. In Irenaeus we can already see the basic outline of a biblical canon from Genesis to Revelation. A right handling of the Scriptures will honor this overarching narrative shape.

At the center of it all is Jesus Christ. One of Irenaeus's favorite concepts is "recapitulation" or "summing up," a term drawn from Eph 1:10, which says that all things in heaven and on earth are gathered up (*anakephalaiōsasthai*) in Christ.[28] According to this concept Jesus Christ's life, death, and resurrection recapitulate or sum up the entire human story from the beginning in Adam until the end, such that Christ both repeats the story of humanity in Adam and also restores what was lost in Adam. By becoming incarnate, Christ, the Word, is the second Adam. Just as the Word first created Adam out of the dust, so the Word in taking flesh upon himself recapitulated Adam; indeed as the Son of Man he in a certain sense comprises Adam, the original man himself.[29] Above all, Christ recapitulated Adam's disobedience and defeat by

---

28. See esp. 1.10.1; 5.20.2; and the references in the following notes. On recapitulation in Irenaeus, see Osborn, *Irenaeus*, 97–140; Gustaf Wingren, *Man and the Incarnation: A Study in the Biblical Theology of Irenaeus* (London: Oliver and Boyd, 1959), 79–90; John Lawson, *The Biblical Theology of Saint Irenaeus* (London: Epworth Press, 1948), 140–98.

29. 3.21.10; 5.14.2; 5.16.3; 5.21.1

the devil. Whereas Adam disobeyed God, was vanquished by the devil, and fell into sin and death by means of a tree, Christ obeyed God unto death, defeated the devil, and freed humanity from sin and death by means of a tree.[30] Christ's temptations and even his birth from a virgin recapitulate Adam's birth and temptation.[31] Christ's death on the sixth day of the week recapitulates Adam's death on the same day of the week.[32] Christ restores the image of God in humanity.[33] He unites humanity with God, and joins the end of the biblical story about God and humanity to its beginning.[34]

(2) The church's Scriptures consist of a single body of writings in Two Testaments, and the Two Testaments are held together by their *united witness* to one God the Father and Creator of all things and to Jesus Christ as the Son of God and the Word through whom the Father created all things. The largest challenge that Irenaeus faced in his struggle against the heresies was the claim that the prophetic and apostolic writings testified not to a single God, but to two gods. Marcion claimed that the God and Father of Jesus Christ was a God of mercy, different from the God of the Jews who was a God of judgment.[35] The Valentinian gnostics taught that Jesus revealed as Father a God who had been unknown to the Jewish people.[36] The Creator God that the Jewish people wor-

---

30. 4.40.3; 5.16.3; 5.19.1; 5.21.1; 5.21.2; 5.23.2; cf. 5.1.1. Also Mary's virginal obedience to the angel recapitulates the disobedience of the virgin Eve (5.19.1).

31. 3.21.10; 5.21.2

32. 5.23.2

33. 5.21.2

34. 3.16.6; 3.18.7; 4.20.4; 5.20.2. Note also that the new covenant of faith (without works of the law) joins the end to the beginning in the faith of Abraham, with the period of the law as an intervening period (4.21.1; 4.25.1; cf. 4.15.1–2 and 4.16.1–5 for the reasons for the intervening period).

35. 1.27.1; 3.25.2–3

36. 1.19.1; 4.6.1

shipped was an inferior divine being, the demiurge, a different Father.[37] Thus the Christ who came to save the gnostics was not the Word of the Creator Father God, but the Word of a previously unknown God. Because this God was not the creator God, he was not concerned to redeem the created world as such, including all humans in both body and soul; he was concerned only to deliver "spiritual" people (that is, the gnostics themselves) from their fleshly entrapment in the material world.[38]

Against these claims, Irenaeus argued strenuously that there is only one God, the one Father and Creator of all things,[39] and there is one Word that became flesh in the person of Jesus Christ, the only-begotten Son of God, who was the very Word of the one Creator God, the God of Israel.[40] The Word became flesh in order to redeem all of humanity, in body and soul, from sin and death and to return all of humanity to God—that is, as we saw above, to recapitulate in himself the story of all of humanity from Adam. Without this basic framework, it is simply not possible to make sense of the received prophetic and apostolic Scriptures. It is for this reason that certain elements—the one Father Creator God; the one Son of God, equated with the Word of the Father, through whom all things were made; the incarnation of the Word in order to redeem humanity from death; and the resurrection of the dead and the final judgment, including punishment of the wicked and salvation of the righteous—feature (along with the Holy Spirit) so prominently in Irenaeus's renditions and allusions to the "rule of truth" as the proper framework for interpreting Scripture.[41] The law,

---

37. 1.5.1

38. 1.6.1

39. Esp. 2.1.1

40. 2.2.5–6; 3.1.2

41. 1.3.6; 1.9.2; 3.11.1; 4.35.4, and esp. 1.10.1; 1.22.1; 3.4.2.

the prophets, the words of the Lord Jesus himself and the apostles bear a common and consistent witness to the unity of God the Father and Creator and to the saving incarnation of the Word. Because the law and the prophets were already utterances of the one Word of the Father, they themselves bear witness to the Word incarnate in Jesus Christ.[43] The law and the gospel have the same author.[44] For his part, Jesus appealed to the law and the prophets as testimony to himself and called as Father the one Creator God and the God of Israel.[45] A right handling of Scripture will respect the unity of the Two Testaments as a coherent testimony to the one Father God, creator of heaven and earth, and to the one Word of the Father incarnate.

(3) *The whole and the parts* of Scripture are to be properly related to each other. Because the Scriptures have a common, divine authorship, the whole and the parts can and must be related to each other. Irenaeus accuses the gnostics of taking texts out of context and twisting their meanings to adapt them to their gnostic ideology.[46] He is especially critical of the gnostics' symbolical and allegorical interpretations of Scripture, because once one has left behind the literal meaning of texts, one can make texts to mean symbolically or allegorically whatever one wants.[47] The gnostics exploit the less clear parts of Scripture for their ideology, while they ignore the parts of Scripture that are clear and harmonious, thereby "braiding ropes of sand."[48] Moreover, the gnostics put the

---

42. 2.9.1; 2.30.6; 2.35.2, 4; 3.9.1–3; 3.10.1–6; 3.11.1–9; 3.12.1–15; 3.16.1–9; 4.20.4; 4.32.1

43. 4.6.6; 4.9.1; 4.10.1; 4.12.4

44. 4.12.3

45. 3.16.5; 4.1.1; 4.2.5; 4.5.2

46. 1.1.3; 1.3.6; 1.8.1; 1.9.2; 2.10.1; 2.20.1; 5.13.5

47. 2.24.3; 2.25.1

48. 1.3.6; 1.8.1; 2.10.1

Scriptures out of order and fail to see the harmony of the whole. To illustrate the point he uses the analogy of some-one who deconstructs a mosaic of a king, rearranges the pieces into the image of a dog or a fox, and then deceives the unsuspecting into believing that it is an image of the king.[49] Another analogy is someone who makes a cento, that is, rear-ranges lines from Homeric verse to form a new poem. To the unsuspecting the new, rearranged poem sounds plausible enough, but it no longer has the same theme as the original.[50] So also the gnostics disfigure the Scriptures by putting them out of order, creating a different theme.

For the right treatment of Scripture Irenaeus speaks of respect for the "body of truth."[51] There is a "body of truth," harmonious in its members, that comes forth from the clearest parts of Scripture. One does not read any part of the Scrip-tures apart from that body so as to invent new truths con-trary to the Scriptures; rather, the "lover of truth" will reflect on how each part relates to the whole and will read every part of Scripture in right relationship to the whole.[52] The less clear parts of Scripture will be interpreted in congruence with the more clear.[53] The clear literal meaning of the Scriptures

---

49. 1.8.1

50. 1.9.4

51. 2.27.1. On the "body of truth" in Irenaeus, see Dominic Unger, *St. Irenaeus: Against the Heresies* (Ancient Christian Writers 55; Volume 1, Book 1; New York: The Newman Press, 1992), 182–83 n. 24.

52. 1.8.1; 1.9.2, 4; 1.10.3; 2.25.1; 2.28.1; 4.33.8; and esp. 4.33.15. The "lover of truth" is one who appreciates how "the whole" hangs together and who respects the relationship between the parts to each other and to the whole. See Irenaeus's lovely image for this in 2.25.2. See also 2.27.1, 3.

53. 2.10.1. For Irenaeus Scripture interprets Scripture. The claim that for Irenaeus "Scripture is ultimately subject to the criterion of tradition, of the doctrine of the Church, of the Rule of Truth itself" (so Dominic Unger in his introduction to *St. Irenaeus: Against the Heresies*, 1.10) seems to be wrong, since for Irenaeus the Rule of Truth itself resides in Scrip-ture (4.35.4). It is the case for Irenaeus that "the Scriptures are not always clear" (ibid., 10), but that fact does not give precedence to tradition, since

that constitutes this "body" has priority over symbolical or allegorical readings.[54] Particularly important for Lutherans, the law of Moses and the doctrine of the gospel are not opposed to each other; one must examine their relationship to each other, which involves both difference and unity and harmony.[55]

Of these principles one might ask, "Who is Irenaeus to decide such things?" But Irenaeus did not develop these principles in an arbitrary way. Rather, they arose from the received documents themselves—from the Scriptures of Israel and from the earliest, most reliable apostolic writings. Although the Jewish canon of Scripture was still in flux at the time of Jesus, it is clear that the basic outlines of a biblical canon, including the law, the prophets, and the Psalms, were in place in the Jewish communities. Jesus, Paul, and the authors of the gospels appealed to those Scriptures as normative and authoritative for a proper understanding of the gospel. Thus the patterns that Irenaeus followed to relate the gospel to the Scriptures of Israel within a coherent biblical framework already existed in the earliest and most reliable apostolic writings. That is why those patterns were to remain normative for the church.

The principles that we have considered have important practical consequences for how one handles Scripture. I will mention just one of them to illustrate the point.

---

unclear parts of Scripture are explained through the clear parts, and a wrong tradition can pervert the meaning of the Scriptures (3.2.1). Scripture and correct tradition (the Rule of Truth) have basically the same doctrinal content (cf. 3.1.2 with 3.4.1–2). See Hans von Campenhausen, *Formation*, 182, 190, 208 n. 295; Osborn, *Irenaeus*, 172; and Hans-Jochen Jaschke, "Irenäus von Lyon," *TRE* 16.258–68, here 261.

54. 2.25.1; 2.27.1–3. Irenaeus himself occasionally gives a symbolic or allegorical reading, but it is normed by the literal meaning of the whole of Scripture, the rule of truth (e.g., 2.24.1–2 and 2.25.1; 5.17.3; 5.20.2).

55. 3.12.12–15

Respect for the unity of the biblical canon, its overall shape, and the right relationship between the whole and the parts requires that, when it comes to discerning how the gospel relates to the law, we are not to rely on our own ideas. Nor are we to make facile judgments about the law, as, for example, when it is said that, since the gospel has abolished the food laws for Christians, it has also abolished laws relating to sexuality and marriage. Not so. On the contrary, as we saw in the case of the Pastoral Epistles, we need to examine carefully the patterns already set by Jesus and apostolic tradition for relating the gospel to the Old Testament, Jesus' teaching, and apostolic teaching. If the Word that became incarnate in Jesus Christ is the Word that already spoke in the law and the prophets,[56] then the incarnate Christ guides us in discerning how the law continues to apply in the Christian life. In any particular case the church must observe how Jesus and the apostles treated the matter and why; for the reasons are discernible, and they did not act arbitrarily.[57] Irenaeus already does this when he writes carefully about which commandments of the law Jesus renewed, which he abolished, and which he deepened, also pointing out that Jesus rebuked those who allowed human precepts and traditions to render the law of God of no effect. Commandments which appear in both the old covenant and the new covenant are not abolished.[58] A right handling of the Word cannot obscure that point.

---

56. See at n. 43 above.

57. E.g., food laws are abolished on the basis of Jesus' teaching (Mark 7:19) and the doctrine of creation (1 Tim 4:1–5; cf. 1 Cor 10:25–26); Jesus' teaching on divorce and remarriage sharpens the Old Testament law because it gives precedence to God's will in creation over the law of Moses; commandments regarding idolatry and sexual immorality are considered to be universally binding (Acts 15, based on Leviticus 17–18), and are also grounded Christologically (e.g., 1 Cor 6:12–20; 10:14–22).

58. 4.12.1–5; 4.13.1–4; 4.15.1–2; 4.16.1–4; cf. 4.28.2. In this way Irenaeus allows the shape of the biblical canon itself to be the controlling factor in determining how the Old Testament law continues to apply to Christians, rather than relying on human opinions. Also to be rejected therefore is an

In sum, we see that Irenaeus insisted, as much as the author of the Pastoral Epistles did, that the gospel must be put in a right relationship to the Scriptures of Israel and to the apostolic tradition. Irenaeus shows himself to have been a faithful practitioner of "rightly handling the word of truth" as put forth in the Pastoral Epistles. One might even say that Irenaeus did for the larger body of writings that would constitute the greater part of the New Testament something like what the author of the Pastoral Epistles himself had done for the gospel at an earlier time. In that respect, at least, Irenaeus is worthy of the greatest respect as well as emulation.

The Problem of the Canon:
Luther and the Confessions on
"Rightly Dividing Law and Gospel"
– A Right Handling of the Word of Truth?

We have noted that the Lutheran Confessions interpret *orthotomein ton logon tes aletheias* in 2 Tim 2:15 in the sense of "rightly distinguishing [or dividing] law and gospel." As Lutherans we need to acknowledge that this is an idiosyncratic interpretation. In fact, honesty requires us to ask whether the Lutheran interpretation of the phrase is justifiable. That *orthotomein* should be interpreted in the sense of "rightly cutting" (the word of truth) is generally not accepted today,[59] and there is no indication that the author of the Pas-

---

approach that attempts to find a mix of divine and human commandments in the law of Moses, such as the Gnostic Ptolemy apparently did (*Letter to Flora*, preserved in Epiphanius of Salamis, *The Panarion*, 33). The solution to the relationship of law and gospel that honors the whole law as Word of God lies in a concept of salvation history. See Campenhausen, *Formation*, 81–87, 165–67.

59. It was once proposed that the verb *orthotomein* might be drawn, e.g., from masonry, so that the verb would mean something like to cut according to the right rule, so as to fit one's speech rightly into the whole edifice of truth. See, e.g., R. St John Parry, *The Pastoral Epistles* (Cambridge: Cambridge University Press, 1920), 57–58. See also J.H. Bernard, *The Pastoral*

toral Epistles actually has "law and gospel" in view, expect perhaps in the broadest sense that we have discussed above, where the gospel is to be rightly related to the Old Testament Scriptures (as well as to the total deposit of apostolic tradition).[60] Have Lutherans inappropriately read a law-gospel hermeneutic into 2 Tim 2:15? The question becomes especially pressing when we recall that Luther exercised a kind of Christological canon criticism in the name of the gospel: Luther doubted the canonicity of certain books in the New Testament, namely, Hebrews, James, Jude, and Revelation, since they did not teach clearly the gospel of justification by faith without works of the law. Does a Lutheran approach to Scripture lead us to violate the canon? That provocative question offers a convenient entrée to a consideration of the problem of the right handling of Scripture in Lutheran perspective.

We should observe first of all that the Lutheran distinction between law and gospel and between their respective functions does have a biblical exegetical basis. The origin of Luther's law/gospel hermeneutic lies in 2 Cor 3:6, where Paul states that "the letter kills, but the Spirit gives life." This verse served as the basis for different hermeneutical theories in the ancient and medieval church. It is no surprise, therefore, that it also becomes a basis for Luther's hermeneutic.[61] As 3:7–11

Epistles (Cambridge: Cambridge University Press, 1899), 122: "rightly dividing the word of truth." "The image here seems rather to be that of a man *cutting* the [word of truth] into its *right* pattern, the standard provided being the Gospel." But such a sense is not supported by linguistic usage.

60. The Pastoral Epistles are, of course, concerned about the right use of the law in relationship to the gospel (1 Tim 1:7–11; cf. 2 Tim 3:16; Titus 1:10–16), but 1 Tim 1:7–11 is not concerned about *distinguishing* law and gospel.

61. For the development of Luther's hermeneutic, see Gerhard Ebeling, "Die Anfänge von Luthers Hermeneutik," *Zeitschrift für Theologie und Kirche* 48 (1951), 172–230; reprinted in his *Lutherstudien I* (Tübingen: J.C.B. Mohr [Paul Siebeck], 1971), 1–68. The article was translated and published in three parts by Richard B. Steele, Franz Posset, and Wilhelm Linss as "The Beginnings of Luther's Hermeneutics," *Lutheran Quarterly* 7/2 (1993), 129–58; 7/3 (1993), 315–38; and 7/4 (1993), 451–68. Citations will follow the English translation.

shows, the "letter" is identifiable with the (Old Testament) law and the Spirit with the gospel, or rather the Spirit's work through the ministry of the gospel. Thus to be aware of a distinction between law and gospel is biblical, proper, and important. We must note, however, that Paul is speaking of letter and Spirit in salvation-historical terms and is not proffering a general biblical hermeneutic.[62] It is problematic, therefore, to use the distinction between law and gospel in a rigid way to reduce all of Scripture to these two items alone, to "killing law" and "life-giving Spirit [gospel]."

The Confessions do teach, it is true, that one can "divide" or "distribute" Scripture into two topics, law and gospel (promise).[63] And Luther's doctrine of law and gospel originates in his grappling with the problem of the relationship between the Testaments and in his attempt to unite the Two Testaments under a single principle of interpretation by way of the concepts letter and Spirit. So law-gospel does allow Luther to develop a single principle for the interpretation of Scripture.[64] But it is doubtful that we can regard law-gospel as an *exhaustive* Lutheran hermeneutic. One can see in the Confessions that the law-gospel hermeneutic functions primarily to fortify the doctrine of justification by faith without works of the law.[65] The purpose of rightly distinguishing law and gospel is to help the preacher keep justification linked to

---

62. The word *pneuma* here is clearly a reference to the Holy Spirit (cf. Rom 7:6; 8:2), so that the verse is a dubious basis for a hermeneutical theory of the letter and the spirit, the latter understood as hidden textual *meaning*. Of course Paul himself offers an important hermeneutical principle in 2 Cor 3:14–16, but it is hardly clear that Paul intends 3:6 to be understood in that sense.

63. See esp. Ap. 4.5; further 4.102, 186. On the development of this approach in Luther, see Rudolf Mau, "Gesetz V," *Theologische Realenzyklopädie* 13.82–90, here 82.

64. Ebeling, "Beginnings," 326–33. See further Mau, "Gesetz V," 82.

65. Ap. 4.5; FC Ep. 5.7; FC SD 5.22. See also my comments and references in "Holy Scripture and Word of God," 103 n. 70.

faith and promise, and to ensure that both law and gospel are heard.[66] This primary function of the law-gospel hermeneutic, to fortify the doctrine of justification, entails that law-gospel, although an important hermeneutical key for Lutherans, cannot be regarded as the only hermeneutical framework for a right handling of Scripture.

The danger of using exclusively a law-gospel hermeneutic is clear. A preacher and teacher who uses only a law-gospel hermeneutic can all too easily adopt a merely *functional* view of Scripture—the Word "kills and makes alive"—while the actual *content* of Scripture becomes optional. Scripture does much more than "kill and make alive." It gives guidance for the ethical life (i.e., the third use of the law).[67] It also has much to teach about anthropology, the world, the church, the sacraments, and other things. Little of these topics can be made to fit into a law-gospel hermeneutical box. If we ignore these other things that Scripture has to teach us, then we will fail to teach "the whole counsel of God" (Acts 20:27) and the total body of biblical truth in doctrine and morals that we are called to preach and to teach.

There is also the danger of falling into a kind of gospel reductionism where the *only* certain thing that the church has to preach and teach is the gospel. That happens, for example, when Article VII of the Augsburg Confession is interpreted to mean that the only thing required for church unity is agreement on the gospel and the sacraments in a narrow sense. "Gospel freedom" can then become an abstract principle that allows one to deconstruct the doctrinal and moral authority of biblical texts. While it may be true that *consentire de doctrina evangelii* in the *satis est* clause of Article VII was not originally meant in the sense of requiring agreement on matters of

---

66. See esp. FC V.

67. Cf. on these points the remarks of Robert W. Jenson, *Lutheran Slogans: Use and Abuse* (Delhi: ALPB Books, 2011), 34–36.

doctrine, it can hardly mean that the gospel can be extracted from the whole body of orthodox doctrine and then be regarded as sufficient for the unity of the church.[68] After all, Article VII itself follows the doctrinal content of the ecumenical creeds (Articles I and III) as well as the doctrine of original sin and the new obedience that does the works commanded by God (Articles II and VI).[69] There is no place in the Lutheran Church for a "gospel" that floats, as it were, disembodied over the canon of Scripture as a whole. From the beginning the church has understood that

---

68. Agreement on the *doctrina evangelii* is in the first instance agreement on the pure preaching of the gospel ("daß da einträchtiglich nach reinem Verstand das Evangelium gepredigt"). The point is not that nothing else in Scripture is important (see the next note). Rather, the article is explicit in rejecting the necessity of agreement on *human traditions*. Those must not be allowed to obscure the gospel (cf. CA 28.77). See Leif Grane, *Die Confessio Augustana: Einführung in die Hauptgedanken der lutherischen Reformation* (Göttingen: Vandenhoeck & Ruprecht, 1990), 76–77; Regin Prenter, *Das Bekenntnis von Augsburg* (Erlangen: Martin-Luther-Verlag, 1980), 107; Harding Meyer and Heinz Schütte, "Die Auffassung von Kirche im Augsburgischen Bekenntnis," Harding Meyer and Heinz Schütte, eds., *Confessio Augustana. Bekenntnis des einen Glaubens: Gemeinsame Untersuchung lutherischer und katholischer Theologen* (Paderborn: Verlag Bonifacius-Druckerei/Frankfurt: Verlag Otto Lembeck, 1980), 168–97, here 195–96; Gunther Wenz, *Theologie der Bekenntnisschriften der evangelisch-lutherischen Kirche: Eine historische und systematische Einführung in das Konkordienbuch* (2 vols.; Berlin: Walter de Gruyter, 1996–98), 2.307, 313–14. Wenz (p. 312) further states that CA VII does not mean that doctrinal propositions are not unimportant, only that they should serve the gospel of justification by grace through faith.

69. Holsten Fagerberg, *A New Look at the Lutheran Confessions* (1529–1537) (tr. G.J. Lund; St. Louis: Concordia Publishing House, 1972), 270–73, and Edmund Schlink, *Theology of the Lutheran Confessions* (tr. P.F. Koehneke and H.J.A. Bouman; Philadelphia: Fortress Press, 1961), 206, emphasize more strongly than others that agreement on *doctrina evangelii* is in effect agreement in creed and confession (contrast Grane in the previous note), though they also recognize that the gospel of justification is at the center of concern. For Fagerberg, *doctrina evangelii* is the same as *doctrina apostolorum*. Schlink (p. 207 n. 13) sees something of a shift from the norm of the gospel in the Augsburg Confession to the formal norm of Holy Scripture in the Formula of Concord.

such a treatment of the gospel ultimately leads to a per-version of the gospel.

In sum, the law-gospel hermeneutical framework, as important as it is, cannot be set against the primary herme-neutical framework of the canon itself. The Lutheran church's doctrinal and moral teaching presupposes a coherent canoni-cal reading of Scripture. Ordained Lutheran pastors are confessionally bound to "rightly distinguish law and gospel." Making this distinction rightly is biblically justified, and it is indispensable for upholding the doctrine of justification by faith without works of the law. But to reduce the "right han-dling of the word of truth" to the distinction between law and gospel in such a way as to make the total *content* of the Scriptural witness optional would be to do the very thing that 2 Tim 2:15 actually aims to prevent. That verse aims to ensure that ministers in the church *rightly relate* the gospel to the total prophetic and apostolic witness, not to make the latter optional on the pretext that doing so is necessary to protect the purity of the gospel. "Rightly distinguishing [or dividing] law and gospel" is an important part of "rightly handling the word of truth," because when one makes the necessary distinction between law and gospel one rightly re-lates gospel to law. But distinguishing law and gospel cannot be the whole of rightly handling the word of truth. That requires fundamental respect for the content and the shape of the biblical canon.

If the whole canon of Scripture is the proper frame-work within which the right distinction of law and gospel is to function, then that raises the question of the coherence and integrity of the canon itself. The topic of the canon has, to put it mildly, not been without controversy in Lutheran history. We have already noted Luther's Christological canon criticism: for the sake of the Pauline gospel of justification, James can be dismissed. Besides the tension between Paul and James, one could cite the tension between Paul and Matthew, the latter holding a stringent view of the necessity of works for salvation (contrast Rom 10:9 with Matt 5:20; 7:21).[70] Does the canon threaten to dissolve into a mass of self-contradictory or incoherent texts? Does the concept of a canon actually work for Lutherans? Does our commitment to the gospel conflict with the canon concept? Those questions bring me to the next section.

The Primacy of the Canon: What Does Respecting the Content and Shape of the Canon Entail?

Given the problems that the canon has presented for Lutherans, we must ask what respecting the content and shape of the canon as the primary hermeneutical framework for the right handling of Scripture entails. I have dealt with some aspects of this question in greater detail elsewhere.[71] Here I limit myself to five comments that I believe are pertinent to the present topic.

(1) The Lutheran Church can only claim to belong to the one, holy, catholic, and apostolic church, and serious ecumenical engagement with other churches will only be possible, if the Lutheran Church is able to make the whole of the Old and New Testament canon of Scripture function as the basis for authoritative teaching. Otherwise we become a sect. Of course, even commitment to the canon does not solve every problem: One can ask, "Which canon? The Roman Catholic canon or the Orthodox canon or the Protestant canon?" Nonetheless, if we remain with those books

---

70. Romans 10:9: "If you confess with your lips that Jesus is Lord and believe in your heart that God raised him from the dead, you will be saved." Matthew 7:21: "Not everyone who says to me, 'Lord, Lord,' will enter the kingdom of heaven, but only the one who does the will of my Father in heaven."

71. Much of the following is worked out in detail in my "Holy Scripture and Word of God," esp. 57–92.

that have received ecumenical acceptance, the Lutheran Church may not unilaterally declare certain books or parts of books of Scripture to be non-authoritative and expect to find ecumenical respect, any more than the Lutheran Church would tolerate, for example, the summary dismissal of the Pauline corpus. Nor does it mean that there will be no disagreement on how one evaluates the *relative* authority of different parts of the canon. How, for example, does one weigh the relative authority of James and Paul, or Matthew and Paul? Here, at times, there may be legitimate disagreement between communions, which must be worked through ecumenically. It is quite a different matter, however, when one church simply ignores texts, effectively declaring certain texts to be non-authoritative by unilateral fiat. That, I fear, is what the ELCA did with its 2009 social statement on human sexuality, when it not only does not comment on, but does not even mention, the biblical texts relating to same-sex intercourse.

(2) Our Confessions point us the way in claiming the whole canon as authoritative Scripture. Despite Luther's Christological canon criticism, the Confessions themselves move in the direction of claiming the whole canon of Holy Scripture for the evangelical cause. Books that proved to be problematic for Lutheran theology, because they seemed to contradict the chief article of justification by grace through faith without works of the law (e.g., Tobit; James), are claimed for the evangelical cause and are integrated into the doctrinal framework. The specific solutions that the Lutheran Confessions offer for integrating James (to take an example) may not today be totally satisfying. In my view, however, the Confessions show the right way, and insights from Lutheran Orthodoxy and historical criticism (see the next point) can assist a confessional approach.

(3) Respect for the overall *shape* of the canon and the place of each book within it can help resolve some of the challenges that the canon itself presents. For example, in

Lutheran Orthodoxy (at least in its early period), the ranking of New Testament books into proto-canonical and deutero-canonical helps resolve some of the tensions within the canon, in that only the former are to establish doctrine.[72] Insofar as the ranking reflects the known history of the New Testament books and their fortunes during the process of canon formation, such a ranking seems appropriate and helpful. So, for example, James, whose canonicity was questioned in the early church, does not have to be dismissed from the canon, but it can comfortably take a back seat to Paul, whose teaching on justification will be normative. Likewise, the more bizarre elements in the eschatology of the book of Revelation can take a back seat to mainstream New Testament eschatology, even while we appreciate Revelation's important function as one of the two bookends of the biblical canon. It is worth noting that the New Testament already offers a certain ranking of Old Testament Scripture (i.e., the law and the prophets with the Psalms are cited as major authorities, whereas the rest of the writings seem to take a back seat), so that we have a Scriptural precedent for this approach to the canon. One might hope that such an approach could receive ecumenical recognition.

Modern study of the New Testament can help us further as we think about the shape of the canon. For example, it has become clear, I think, that James's teaching on justification, namely, that one is justified not by faith alone but by faith and works, must be understood, in part, as a reaction to a misunderstood Paulinism (in the direction of antinomianism or libertinism; cf. 2 Peter 3:15–17), and, in part, as addressing a different issue from Paul.[73] For its part, Matthew is only

---

72. See, e.g., the citations in Heinrich Schmid, *The Doctrinal Theology of the Evangelical Lutheran Church* (tr. C.A. Hay and H.E. Jacobs; 4th ed.; Philadelphia: Lutheran Publication Society, 1899), 80–91.

73. See, e.g., John Reumann, *Righteousness in the New Testament* (Philadelphia: Fortress Press/New York: Paulist Press, 1982), 155–58.

one of four canonical Gospels and must be read within the fourfold Gospel. In this fourfold Gospel the gospel of salvation by faith is clearly enunciated by Jesus (John 11:25–26; cf. 6:29). Matthew's rigorism does not stand alone as a representation of Jesus' teaching on salvation, and should not be used that way.[74] Matthew can be seen as preserving the gospel for law-observant Jewish-Christians, whom Paul accepts with ecumenical respect (Rom 14:1–15:13; Gal 2:7–9), although he would vociferously reject any notion that the Jewish-Christian can rely on works of the law for justification (Rom 4:12). In addition, Matthew's and James's rigorism stands as a constant and needed reminder that, although the law has come to an end as the means to justification before God (Rom 10:4), God's law remains the standard for Christian life. When the Confessions uphold a third use of the law, they show respect for the overall shape of the canon. The ethical rigorism of Matthew and James takes its proper place in relationship to the gospel of justification. A third use of the law is neither a false way to salvation nor a denial of evangelical freedom. Rather the law provides the structure for the proper exercise of Christian freedom.[75]

(4) The chief doctrinal content of Scripture—that is, what is to be held as binding teaching in faith and morals—is summarized in the articles of faith in the ecumenical creeds as well as in the Confessions. These articles also establish the unity of Scripture. The Lutheran Confessions treat Scripture

---

74. Note also that the Gospel narratives (including Matthew) contain within themselves an answer to the perplexing problem of how anyone can be saved on the basis of ethical perfection: "For mortals it is impossible [to be saved], but for God all things are possible" (Matt 19:26). The disciples' failure to follow Jesus (26:31) will be met with the risen Christ's (reconciling) presence (26:32; 28:20).

75. In this way Matthew preserves the essential biblical insight, beginning already in Genesis 2, that God's law is given originally to shape human freedom that is open to eternal life with God. That point should not be obscured.

as a coherent and unified body of writings and offer patterns for treating it as such.[76]

(5) Moreover, the articles of faith can serve as trustworthy guides in orientation to which one may submit disputes over biblical texts where clarity may be lacking, or where for various reasons different voices in the canon compete for primacy.[77] The articles of faith help us set the right accents in our interpretation and use of Scripture, without, on the one hand, falling into a wooden literalism or fundamentalism, and, on the other hand, without deconstructing the canon of Scripture as a unified authority.

In conclusion, a "right handling of the word of truth" from a Lutheran perspective will respect the overall shape of the canon. In continuity with the Pastoral Epistles and Irenaeus, it will keep in view the total context and the total body of teaching on faith and morals that is found in the canon of the Old and New Testament Scriptures. The apt preacher and teacher will prevent distortions of the gospel by neither obscuring the gospel of justification in the strict sense nor by turning "gospel freedom" into an instrument for deconstructing the total prophetic and apostolic witness of Scripture in which the gospel is embedded and apart from which it makes no sense.

The Promise of the Canon

I would like to end with a word of encouragement. I have written at length about some of the problems that the canon of Scripture presents. But I want to end by lifting up the promise of the canon.

---

76. I give examples in "Holy Scripture and Word of God," 70–72.

77. For examples, see "Holy Scripture and Word of God," 90–92, as well as my essay, "Canon, Creeds, and Confessions: An Exercise in Lutheran Hermeneutics," *Lutheran Theological Journal* 46/1 (2012): 26–50.

We live in difficult times. Those who dare to uphold the authority of Scripture in its canonical form can expect today to be called bigoted, hateful, unenlightened, authoritarian, uncompassionate, and narrow-minded. Let us not be put off by that! Commitment to truth often brings with it suffering. But when one suffers for commitment to truth, that person is blessed (cf. 1 Pet 2:20; 3:14; 4:14). We should remain confident that, in meeting the challenges of today and in the future, holding fast to Scripture as a canon, that is, as a standard or measure (*kanōn*) of truth, will stand us in good stead for the long haul. That is what I mean by the *promise* of the canon. I am deeply convinced that the canon of Scripture, if we respect its canonical *shape*, will remain a sure and reliable guide for the church in all matters of faith, doctrine, and morals as we face the challenges of the present day and in the future, as it has done for the church in the past.

Respect for the canon of Scripture, in the totality of the prophetic and apostolic witness, does not imply an unthinking "fundamentalistic" reception of Scripture from beginning to end. In fact, it implies just the opposite. One of the main shortcomings of fundamentalism is that, because it tends to treat Scripture in a flat two-dimensional way, it has no way of seriously grappling with contradiction, the historically conditioned nature of biblical texts, or the possibility that different biblical texts may vary in their relative authority. Reaction against fundamentalism, together with the rise of modern historical consciousness, a modern scientific worldview, and historical criticism of the Bible, leads many people today to assume that the only possible way forward is to adopt an eclectic view of the Bible, where we choose to honor those parts of Scripture that suit us, our biases, and our worldview, while we feel free to dismiss the rest. Serious Lutherans need to realize that such an approach can only lead in one direction: to the dissolution of the church's confessional foundations, ultimately including the doctrine of justification by faith itself; for Paul's teaching on justification already presupposes a coherent canon concept.[78] If we deconstruct the canon, what will prevent us finally from deconstructing the doctrine of justification? As I have argued here and elsewhere, a more promising way forward is to honor the *shape* of the canon, paying attention to such things as: the overarching narrative of the canon; the unity of the Two Testaments; the relationship between the whole and the parts of Scripture; patterns found in Scripture itself for rightly relating the gospel to the rest of Scripture, and particularly to the law; hearing the different voices in Scripture, each on its own terms (even when they seem to contradict or stand in tension with each other), and assessing their relative authority; and allowing the church's articles of faith, which themselves presuppose a coherent canon of Scripture, to guide one in discerning which parts of Scripture are non-negotiable and which are not.[79]

It will be helpful to give an example of what I mean by the promise of the canon. My example will seek to illustrate what it means rightly (and wrongly) to relate the gospel to the rest of the canon. At the same time it will seek to illustrate in more general terms what it means to respect the shape of the canon along the lines given in the last paragraph.

In many versions of liberal Protestantism today, the gospel is extracted from the canon of Scripture and is treated as an abstract principle of freedom. This principle of "gospel freedom" can then be used as an instrument for deconstructing normative structures, whether they be normative structures of doctrine (e.g., the doctrine of the Trin-

---

78. This canon concept includes an overarching narrative framework; the congruence of law and gospel within God's overall plan; and a right relationship between the whole and the parts (e.g., Romans 4; Galatians 3).

79. For examples of such an approach, see my "Holy Scripture and Word of God," 83–92.

ity), or normative structures for human life (e.g., marriage). The problem is illustrated well in the case that I cited at the beginning of the paper: the claim from an ELCA pastor that there is no biblical norm for marriage. Gospel freedom enables us to make of marriage and human sexuality what we will.

It is, in fact, in the realm of marriage and sexuality that this problem is playing itself out most clearly. Secular feminism, gender ideology, and the same-sex marriage movement, at least in some manifestations, teach men and women that there is no significant difference between man and woman, and that there are no normative structures for shaping their relationships with one another. Men and women should be able to shape their lives any way they want, in whatever permutations of sexual relationships they want—"as long as no one gets hurt," as the saying goes. Protestant churches underwrite this agenda to the extent that they allow an abstract principle of gospel freedom to be co-opted by a foreign ideology and allow that foreign ideology to deconstruct their own canonical Scriptures.

The ideology sounds liberating. But at some point people run up against the truth that men and women are different, and that the differences matter. While promising liberation, ideological feminism all too often leads to new oppressions. It claims to defend a woman's right to the freedom of her own body, primarily through a regime of artificial contraception and abortion; yet, ironically, the result all too often is that women are *trapped*—with unintended and unwanted pregnancies, often abandoned by men who have been taught that fathers are not needed, perhaps not even wanted. The dreamed-of freedom becomes unfreedom. The culture of sexual liberation was supposed to put women on an equal playing field with men—women should be able to behave as badly as men. Yet in those places where radical feminism and gender ideology are strongest, namely, on college campuses, where one might expect women's liberation to be most advanced, the so-called hook-up culture is making women into objects of male sexual predation as never before.

Might we dare to suggest that respect for the biblical canon as a measure of truth can help meet the challenges of our day? The idea that humans can, this side of heaven, transcend sexual difference is a gnostic idea, not a canonical one. When we look at the Old Testament, we find in the creation stories that man and woman *both* constitute an originary unity (Gen 1:27; 2:21–23) *and* exist in a relationship of difference and mutuality (1:28; 2:24). The one-flesh sexual union of man and woman in (lifelong) marriage (Gen 2:24; cf. Mark 10:6–9) signifies at once both their unity and their difference. Both aspects must be kept in view.

The New Testament's view of reality affirms and fulfills both aspects of the Old Testament view of the relationship between man and woman. On the one hand, Jesus teaches that the resurrected dead, like angels, no longer marry or are given in marriage (Mark 12:25). In a certain sense, then, eternal life for man and woman means a return to their originary unity, where sexual difference is transcended. But since sexual difference and marriage of man and woman belong to God's creation, they remain God's normative institution as long as the created order endures, until the last day. Although Jesus and (following him) Paul recognize the legitimacy and indeed the gift of the single celibate life for the sake of the kingdom of God (Matt 19:10–12; 1 Cor 7:7–8, 40), they also honor God's institution of marriage of man and woman (Mark 10:2–9; 1 Corinthians 7). Thus the renunciation of marriage in their own lives cannot be seen as a *premature transcendence* of the created difference between male and female (as in gnosticism) but only as an anticipation of life in the world to come, where Christ will be joined to us and we to Christ. There will indeed be marriage in heaven, but it will be the marriage of God's saints to Christ the Lamb (Rev 19:7). Christ is the second Adam, and we the church will be his Eve. This marriage, of course, will not be sexual, although it will entail a depth of intimacy that we can now only barely imagine. In this marriage unity and difference will be preserved and transformed. We will be deeply and eternally united with Christ, and yet he will also continue to be our head, the eternal Son of God, the Bridegroom. Eternal life with Christ will both preserve and utterly transform the unity and difference that we know now as man and woman and that is grounded in God's creation. Thus both the single life and marriage of man and woman, each in its own way, anticipate our marriage to Christ in the world to come.

This brief example illustrates what I mean by respecting the shape of the canon—taking seriously the overarching narrative framework from creation to eschatological redemption, where the end both preserves and transcends the beginning; the unity of the Two Testaments; the relationship of the whole and the parts; and the right relationship between the gospel and the law: the gospel of the kingdom frees the Christian from the Torah's command to marry, but it does not free the Christian from living within God's created order. The shape of the canon teaches the church to see things in right relationship to each other. Both the single life and the married life of man and woman are pleasing to God and are signs of the kingdom. Each in its own way, the single life and the married life of man and woman honor God's created order, which in turn foreshadows the unity and difference that will be our eternal life joined to Christ the Bridegroom in heaven. Eternal union with Christ will fulfill the human's deepest longings for union with the other. The shape of the canon then also teaches men and women to see their own lives in right relationship to each other. Both the single life and the married life of man and woman are good, but neither is an ultimate good. They are both anticipations of an ultimate good.

But, it will be objected, the ethics of sexuality in Scripture is oppressive, especially to women. I ask: is it really so?

Might it not rather be that Scripture takes seriously the reality of being man and woman, and that it offers both men and women true freedom within that reality? I would argue that when Scripture is read as a canonical whole and with respect to its canonical shape, Scripture is not oppressive; it is honest: being a woman entails certain vulnerabilities that do not affect men in quite the same way (1 Peter 3:7). The question, then, for both man and woman, is not how to live as though those vulnerabilities do not exist or as though there were no differences between man and woman, but how to live with those vulnerabilities and differences. And here Scripture has much to teach: about male responsibility (Eph 5:28); about mutuality between man and woman (1 Cor 7:4); and about true freedom, which is not about owning one's body and doing with it whatever one wishes, but about honoring God with one's body in chastity (1 Cor 6:12–20), which applies to both man and woman—there is no double standard here—and living in the true freedom from self and sin that God's Spirit gives (Gal 5:13–26).

That is not to deny that the canon contains texts that can be (mis)used to oppress or mistreat women (1 Tim 5:14; Titus 2:5). But that is nothing unique to Scripture. Any authoritative document, whether that be Scripture, a civil or criminal law, or even a resolution of a churchwide assembly, can be used to mistreat people. And it must be said that Scripture contains a multitude of texts that counter misuse (cf. Eph 5:25–33), texts that highlight the dignity of women and their full humanity (Gen 1:27; Luke 10:38–42) and that teach mutuality (1 Cor 7:4). Respecting the canon of Scripture does not mean adopting a view that women must adopt traditional gender roles. That would be to err just as profoundly as radical feminism errs. (At the same time, we will not ridicule those who choose to adopt traditional gender roles.) Rather, it is a matter of taking seriously all that the canon has to say on the topic of men and women, helping men and women to imagine what such a life looks like, and then inviting them to order their lives according to the sure guideposts that the canon offers.

The church will then teach *both* that persons in Christ transcend the distinction of male and female in baptism in a sense (Gal 3:28) *and* that created sexual difference continues (1 Cor 11:2–16)—not one or the other, but both/and.[80] In fact, it is only when we teach both of these insights together that the truth of each insight is preserved in its integrity. If we teach only that we transcend male and female in Christ, we risk entering flights of fancy removed from reality. On the other hand, if we teach only on-going created sexual difference, we risk losing sight of the biblical vision of mutuality between man and woman. One of the gifts of having a canon of Scripture is that one text can correct the worst excesses that we, as finite and sinful humans, can come up with on the basis of another text. One text limits the meaning of another text and helps us to see its true import. By contrast, when "gospel freedom" is allowed to function apart from the canon as an abstract and absolute principle, it no longer has anything left to correct it, because the gospel no longer resides in its proper context.

The latter is, in effect, the gnostic heresy: the gospel is taken to imply that we have already now transcended—been liberated from—the created order. What is the effect of this heresy? Let the Gnostics speak for themselves:

> Simon Peter said to [the disciples]: "Let Mary go away from us, for women are not worthy of life." Jesus said: "Lo, I shall lead her, so that I may make

---

80. Galatians 3:28 does not mean that men and women cease to exist as men and women in worldly terms, or that the differences between them have been erased (cf. 1 Cor 11:2–16), any more than Paul thought that Christians (of his day) ceased to be identifiable in ethnic terms as Jews or Gentiles (Rom 4:12; chapter 14) or as slave and free (1 Cor 7:21–24), even if such differences lost their significance with respect to baptismal identity and unity.

her a male, that she too may become a living spirit, resembling you males. For every woman who makes herself a male will enter the kingdom of heaven." (*Gospel of Thomas* 114)

Here the biblical vision for man and woman—encompassing both unity and difference, at both beginning and end, and seeing creation and redemption in right relationship to each other: eschatological redemption transcends, but does not prematurely replace, sexual difference—is abandoned for a premature overcoming of sexual difference.[81] Far from bringing freedom, however, premature liberation from the created order promises to bring new oppression: not mutuality of man and woman within the reality of sexual difference, as in the biblical vision, but destruction of difference, largely at the cost of the female.[82] Because Gnosticism denies a canon of Scripture, it has nothing to correct its own worst excesses. Because Gnosticism despises created reality itself, it lacks the resources to guide men and women in living within reality.[83]

---

81. See further *Gospel of Thomas* 22, 106. For commentary on these sayings, see Uwe Karsten-Plisch, *The Gospel of Thomas: Original Text with Commentary* (tr. G.S. Robinson; Stuttgart: Deutsche Bibelgesellschaft, 2008).

82. On the saying 114 and thoughts on how women might have practically implemented such a teaching in antiquity, see Stephen J. Patterson, *The Gospel of Thomas and Jesus* (Sonoma: Polebridge Press, 1993), 153–55, and further references there; and Marvin W. Meyer, "'Male' and 'Female' in the Gospel of Thomas," *New Testament Studies* 31 (1985): 554–70, here 561–67. Even if femaleness in this saying is symbolic for the earthly, mortal, and sensual (so Meyer), the overall tenor is of the overcoming of sexual difference and the devaluing of the woman. In fairness we should note that the idea that woman should become male was found in non-gnostic Christian tradition as well (Patterson, p. 154; Meyer, p. 563). One must ask, however, whether the idea does not go beyond the bounds of canonical biblical Christianity, while it fits very well the gnostic worldview.

83. The example demonstrates the importance of reading the creation stories in Genesis 1 and 2 in canonical unity (even if they have separate origins). At least some gnostics separated Genesis 1 and Genesis 2 (some

Conclusion

I entitled this paper, "On Being 'Lovers of Truth': The Canon of Scripture and the Church's Commitment to Truth," inspired by Irenaeus. This is no place to develop a theological theory of truth. But surely one essential element of truth is that we see things in right relationship to each other. I have argued that a right handling of the word of truth (2 Tim 2:15) means putting the gospel into right relationship to the whole of the prophetic and apostolic witness. More generally, to respect the canon of Scripture means that we will see the various parts of Scripture in right relationship to each other. To be more exact, it is the canon itself that helps us to see things in right relationship to each other.

If as the church we are to love truth, then we must love all truth. We must love not only biblical truth, but also historical truth and scientific truth. The church does not claim to possess in its canon of Scripture truth in every realm of knowledge. The church can rightly claim to possess in its canon of Scripture all that is needed for true teaching in faith and morals, all that the human needs to know about his or her nature and destiny, about his or her eternal salvation, and about how to conduct oneself in this world. In other matters, however, the church will not claim to have such knowledge. Therefore the church will celebrate, and not denigrate,

---

what like Philo) so as to find the ideal bisexual man in 1:26–27 and an earthly man in 2:7 (Irenaeus, *Against the Heresies* 1.18.2). The gnostic distortion of Scripture celebrates bisexuality as characteristic of the higher spiritual elite. In the gnostic myth the ideal human exists as an androgynous soul. The creation of the female is viewed as the result of a primordial fall of the soul. Salvation involves the transcendence of sexual difference already before death and/or entrance into the kingdom of heaven. See Dennis Ronald MacDonald, *There is No Male and Female: The Fate of a Dominical Saying in Paul and Gnosticism* (Philadelphia: Fortress Press, 1987), 36–38, 50–63. A canonical reading of Genesis 1 and 2 reads the two chapters together (and together with the New Testament) and finds there both the unity and the difference of man and woman that constitute their nature in time and eternity.

the geologist's search for truth, and the astronomer's, and the psychologist's, and the historian's, and yes, even the historical critic's search for truth about the Bible. Sometimes their search for truth will present challenges to the church's understanding of things. How will the church respond?

The church should not be afraid to have its canonical texts interrogated, even criticized, from any direction. For that also is a part of loving truth—being willing to receive criticism gracefully, because the critique may well be true and right, and being confident that, if one has really discovered truth, it will withstand scrutiny. But being willing to accept criticism gracefully does not mean adopting a critique uncritically; rather, when critique comes its way, the church goes back to its canonical texts as its measure of truth, re-examines them, and responds accordingly. Sometimes the church will need to change its views on specific controverted points (let me simply mention the case of Galileo here), sometimes it will not. But we should remain confident that the canon of Scripture, when we respect its canonical *shape*, will guide us rightly in all matters of faith, doctrine, and morals.[84]

So let us hold fast to the canon, to the truth of Scripture! The world needs us to do this, even if the world does not know it. As civil society in the West degenerates, its people appear to be bent more and more on denying objective truth and its claim on their lives, bent more and more on denying any truth that transcends the self as measure of truth. The

---

84. The church will not insist that Jos 10:12–13 teaches us astronomical truth, but that does not undermine the doctrine of creation based on Scripture as a whole. The church will honor the critique of same-sex intercourse in Rom 1:26–27, not because Paul explains "scientifically" the cause of homosexual orientation—he does not do so—but because these verses constitute a theological judgment on the immorality of same-sex behavior as an affront to God's creative will, a critique that agrees not only with natural law (1:18–23) but also with the content and shape of Scripture's teaching on marriage and sexuality as a whole.

results of this denial are everywhere to be seen. Although it is easy to become discouraged, we need to remember that no matter how much the people of the West turn away from truth, truth will not turn away from them. The truth about what it is to be a human before God will continue to haunt their consciences and make its claim on them, even against their will. They will hear the voice of truth calling to them, no matter how dimly, as from a distant past. And after people have destroyed themselves by their greed, their selfishness, their lust, their will to power, their nihilism, and their despair, still the Word of God will remain; for the Word of God remains forever, even when people reject it, even when people think to crucify it and bury it. And perhaps we still have reason to hope that the people of the West, even if it is only soul by single soul, will come to realize that the true freedom and life that they are seeking has always been right there, in front of their eyes and in their ears, if they would only see and listen. We must be there for them. It is for their sake, for the sake of a world that is losing its way, but a world that God still deeply loves, that we must be and remain "lovers of truth."

Wrestling Till the Break of Day

How Luther Read the Bible

David S. Yeago

Introduction

It is one of those ironies with which modern history is full. The Bible, which was supposed to be Protestantism's glory and strength, has become its torment. The history of Protestant theology for the past two centuries and more is a story of controversy and division over the nature and authority and interpretation of Scripture. Protestant churches today are wracked with controversies, purportedly about sex but really about how we should read the Bible and what difference it should make to us. Even among Evangelicals, with their historically "high" view of Scripture, there are reports of rising biblical illiteracy while significant evangelical movements seem to be making their own version of the liberal Protestant turn to focus on feelings rather than the word.

This is the context in which I have been asked to speak to you about Martin Luther's way of reading and interpreting Scripture. It is an interesting and oddly challenging assignment. Luther certainly leaves us in no doubt that he regarded himself as first and foremost a *scriptural* theologian. In his own view, everything he wrote was fundamentally exegesis. It may seem strange, then, that the Luther-research of the nineteenth and twentieth centuries found Luther's relationship to the Bible somewhat baffling, and frequently presented his theology in abstraction from his exegetical engagement with biblical texts. The key to his thinking has often been sought in his existential "discovery" of the gospel, as though he was primarily an interpreter of his own experience rather than Scripture. Or else he has been treated not as an exegete but as an extremely badly organized systematic theologian.

In large part this was a result of the protracted Protestant controversy just mentioned. Read from the perspective of this modern conflict, Luther is indeed hard to figure. Attempts to enlist his prestige on the side of one party or the other have regularly led to distorted accounts that are plausible only if one ignores or dismisses large chunks of what Luther actually says and does in his engagement with the Bible. Indeed, both sides have found it difficult to take Luther's exegesis seriously as exegesis, as proper exposition of the biblical texts. Both sides have found his biblical interpretation, particularly of the Old Testament, fanciful and arbitrary; both have tried in vain to find in his hermeneutical and theological *principles* a thread that would lead beyond his *practice* to something more congenial.

Now, this brings us already to a somewhat awkward point. Luther's scriptural interpretation does not cause this discomfort primarily because of something "distinctively Lutheran." The root of the problem is not the law-gospel hermeneutic or the role of the doctrine of justification or the centrality of the notion of promise or anything of that sort. Rather, Luther's engagement with the Bible has been hard to comprehend because it stands outside a set of assumptions about language, meaning, and method that tend to be shared by both modern conservatives and modern liberals. At the same time, as the study of the *pre-modern* tradition of Christian biblical exegesis advances, it is becoming more and more apparent just how thoroughly Luther shared in the fundamental assumptions of a practice of scriptural reading that begins within the New Testament texts themselves and extends through the patristic and medieval eras past Luther into early modern times.

This is awkward because we Lutherans are not accustomed to reading Luther as a representative of a larger tradition. We tend to think of him as a solo act, not a voice in a choir. We are interested in what is "distinctive" about Luther, since we suppose that what makes Luther different from everyone else is what makes Lutherans special. But let me point out the important distinction between what's *distinctive* of Luther and what's *characteristic* of him. Something can be characteristic and very important without being distinctive. It's not distinctive of horses to be warm-blooded quadrupeds, but you would be hard-pressed to understand them if you ignored or denied that fact. It's not distinctive of Lutheranism to confess the faith of the Apostles' Creed, but Lutheranism apart from that creedal substance would be little more than a ghostly remnant.

In the same way, Luther's characteristic assumptions about Scripture are fundamentally those of the whole premodern Christian tradition. Within that framework, he does indeed have "distinctive" insights into the structure and force of the scriptural discourse. But if we simply snatch at those distinctive bits, tearing them out of Luther's own frame of reference and transferring them into our context (as we understand it), then we will be not so much *learning* from Luther as *using* him to advance our own agendas. We will certainly not be facing up to his full challenge to us, and even the "distinctives" we cherish will very likely mean something very different to us from what they meant to him.

Today, therefore, we will encounter a Luther who stands solidly in a tradition, a very old tradition which in a real sense is the ground from which all classic Christian doctrine and theology have grown. That ground was a practice of reading and interpreting Scripture that took shape in the early centuries of the church's life, starting in the New Testament itself.

In this approach to the Bible, as my teacher George Lindbeck once put it, Scripture is read as "a canonically and

narrationally unified and internally glossed (that is, self-refer-
ential and self-interpreting) whole centered on Jesus Christ,
and telling the story of the dealings of the Triune God with
his people and his world in ways that are typologically ...
applicable to the present."[1] That is to say, Luther reads the
Bible as an intricately complex but nonetheless unified literary whole, in which each part bears on the interpretation of
every other part, telling a story that embraces the whole of
space and time. The theme of this great literary composi-
tion, presented in countless variations and from every possible angle, is the mystery of Jesus Christ and the disciple-
ship of his people in the midst of a still-unredeemed world
bent on subverting their faith, hope, and love. For Luther, as
for the tradition in which he stood, to engage the Bible in
this way is to *enter into reality*, to find our place in the true story
of the world, involving a protracted struggle with the manifold distortions of attitude and perception that delude us
and leave us wandering haplessly in a fool's paradise.

Wrestling Jacob

Instead of discussing this further in abstract methodological
terms, I want to look carefully at one extended example,
Luther's exposition of Jacob's wrestling at the Jabbok in
Genesis 32, from his last great work, the *Lectures on Genesis*,
which occupied his last ten years of teaching and now fill the
first eight volumes of the American Edition of *Luther's Works*.[2]

---

1. Lindbeck, "Scripture, Consensus, and Community," *The Church in a Postliberal Age* (Grand Rapids: Eerdmans, 2002), 203.
2. Luther will normally be cited from *Luther's Works*, American Edition (55 vols.; ed. Jaroslav Pelikan and Helmut T. Lehmann; Philadelphia: Muhlenberg and Fortress, and St. Louis: Concordia, 1955-86). Hereafter referred to as *LW*. Occasionally reference will be made to the critical edition: *D. Martin Luthers Werke*. Kritische Gesamtausgabe. 73 vols. Weimar: Herman Böhlaus Nachfolger, 1883-2009. Hereafter referred to as *WA*.

1. Christ in Genesis

Luther's discussion of Jacob's meeting with Esau is typically long and discursive, taking up nearly sixty pages in the English translation.[3] Modern readers will no doubt be relieved at Luther's rejection of Augustine's allegorical reading, according to which Jacob represents simultaneously both the Jewish people, who fought against God in crucifying Christ, and the believing church, which receives the blessing of God. Luther calls this "too hard and forced"; it does not follow the narrative flow of the text, but breaks it, making two different characters of the one character in the story who both struggles and is blessed.[4]

But our relief is likely to be short-lived when we find that Luther takes the *literal*, or as he puts it, the "narrative" sense of the text[5] to be that Jacob wrestled with the Son of God, the one who was to be incarnate for the salvation of the world. Notice: Luther does not take this to be an allegori-

---

3. *LW* 6: 96-155. This includes not only the wrestling-scene but the whole story of Jacob's preparation for his meeting with Esau.

4. *LW* 6:153.

5. *LW* 6:125: According to Luther, Origen and Jerome were unsuccessful in reading this text allegorically because "they did not have a perfect knowledge of the narratives, without which no one can handle allegories successfully. So before all else the historical sense must be dug out. This teaches, consoles, and confirms. Afterwards allegory embellishes and illustrates it as a witness. But the narrative is the author, so to say, or the head and foundation of the matter." Luther's attitude to allegory, in this commentary and elsewhere, is complex. He can say that he "hates" allegory, but at the same time, as here, he can set forth principles of proper allegorizing. Indeed, after rejecting Augustine's allegory, he goes on to offer what he takes to be a proper, narrative-based allegorical reading of the story; cf. LW 6:153-155. It should be noted, though, that what he says about the relationship between the "historical sense" and allegory in the passage cited is thoroughly patristic and traditional. For a substantial challenge to simplistic presentations of Luther as an opponent of figural-allegorical reading, see Johann Anselm Steiger, *Funf Zentralthemen der Theologie Luthers und Seiner Erben: Communicatio-Imago-Figura-Maria-Exempla* (Leiden: Brill, 2002), 147-179.

cal reading, but the text's "simple meaning."[6] Furthermore, he asserts this over against a widespread and apparently more commonsensical exegetical tradition that took the "man" who wrestled with Jacob to be an angel. How can Luther claim that Jesus Christ is a character in this story from Genesis *according to its "narrative" sense?*

To begin with, Luther points out that the text itself makes no mention of any angel. Jacob experiences a long wrestling-match with "a man" (v. 24) but in the end perceives that he has been wrestling with *God*: "I have seen God face to face and yet my life has been preserved" (v. 30).[7] That the wrestler is said to be both "man" and "God" is no accident for Luther, but a significant Christological indicator. Yet his Christological reading does not depend only on the conjunction of humanity and deity in the figure of the wrestler; Luther also discerns a broader pattern of Christological disclosure in Genesis into which this story fits.

Luther refers to his earlier exegesis of the story of Jacob's Ladder in Genesis 28. There, he points out, the Lord who stands on the ladder is not confused with the angels who ascend and descend the ladder, but represents "the Son of God, who was to become incarnate, our Lord Jesus Christ, who is true God and true Man."[8] Luther is of course following the Gospel of John, which identifies the ladder on which the angels ascend and descend with the "Son of Man" (John 1:51). Luther develops the point by way of the Christological doctrine of the communication of attributes: because of the union of deity and humanity in the person of Christ, "the human being is on high above all creatures, and God is the

---

6. *LW* 6:146.

7. Biblical texts are cited from the Revised Standard Version. Alterations to the RSV translation will be noted in parentheses.

8. *LW* 6:126. Luther refers back to his extensive Christological exposition of this text in LW 5.

lowliest one."[9] That is, the "Lord" at the top of the ladder is the man Jesus, and the one who touches earth at the base of the ladder is the eternal Son of God.

Luther applies this Christological logic to the whole phenomenon of *God's* appearances in *bodily* form to the patriarchs: the one who "touches earth" in these appearances, who encounters the ancient saints in visible form at the bottom of the ladder is the eternal Son, true God, the one who was to become incarnate. Luther writes that the Lord Jesus Christ "was very familiar to the holy Fathers and often appeared to them and spoke to them. He exhibited himself to them in such a form that he might testify that he would at some time dwell with us in the form of human flesh."[10] The appearances thus anticipate and prophesy the incarnation that was still historically future to the patriarchs.

Here we see Luther exemplifying in his own way the premodern interpretive consensus described above. Like the whole church before him, Luther takes the Bible to be a unified book, the whole of which bears significantly on the interpretation of each particular passage. The canon as a whole is the relevant context in which the "literal sense" of a particular text is determined.

Furthermore Luther believes that the Bible has an inner structure and design that become manifest in the New Testament. As he says elsewhere, borrowing terms that may reflect the influence of St. Hilary of Poitiers, to understand the *verba*, the words of Scripture, it is necessary to know to what *res*, what reality, the words refer.[11] This has been made known in the resurrection and in the apostolic preaching:

---

9. *LW* 6:126.

10. *LW* 6:144.

11. Cf. Hilary, *De trinitate* IV, 14: "The *res* is not subject to the discourse (*sermo*)" of Scripture, "but the discourse is subject to the *res*." Implicit is the charge that Arian exegesis constructs an illusory *res* from the words of Scripture according to their own preconceived ideas.

"the seal has been broken and the stone rolled away from the tomb, and that supreme mystery has gone forth, that Christ the Son of God has become human, that God is one and triune, that Christ suffered for us and will reign eternally."[12] The whole Bible, with its manifold human authorship, is at the same time what Luther calls "the rhetoric of the Holy Spirit"[13] whose office is to bear witness to this "supreme mystery," the redemptive Trinitarian mystery of Christ.

The relationship of Old and New Testaments in this scheme is one of mutual clarification and illumination. The true significance of the Old Testament is only seen clearly in the light of Christ, but Luther is quite clear that the converse is equally true: *Jesus Christ can only be rightly understood in terms of the Old Testament.* "It is there," in the Old Testament, "that people like us should read and study, drill ourselves, and see what Christ is, for what purpose he has been given, how he was promised, and how all Scripture tends towards him."[14] For Luther that not only means that we should interpret the mission of Jesus in terms of Old Testament themes and concepts. It means that the Old Testament itself *presents* Christ to us in manifold ways, in types and figures, in the prophetic proclamation and elaboration of God's promises and, as in this text, in stories of Christ's *deeds* among his people even before his coming in the flesh.

2. The Tribulation of Jacob

Luther's overtly Christological reading of the story is not the only thing about his exegesis that sits poorly to modern conservative and liberal expectations. Throughout his interpretation, he regularly ascribes feelings and motivations to Jacob of which, he admits, the text says nothing: "...what his dis-

---

12. *De servo arbitrio, WA* 18:609. Cf. LW 33: 25-26.

13. Cf. *Lectures on Genesis Chapters* 15-20, *LW*: 3, 347.

14. Luther, "A Brief Instruction on What to Look for and Expect in the Gospels," *LW* 35:122.

tress of heart was in that struggle is not described. We infer that this selfsame tribulation was a fight of unbelief,"[15] that is, a struggle with despair, with the threatened extinction of confidence in God's promises.

At first glance this seems like the very sort of "psychologizing" against which both conservative and liberal students are warned in their exegesis classes. One might indeed suspect that Luther is merely projecting his own experiences of tribulation or *Anfechtung* onto the text. Yet here too a closer look complicates the picture. Luther turns out to have *reasons* for "inferring" that the inner meaning of Jacob's wrestling is the struggle of trusting faith against despair.

Luther argues that his reading has a basis in the text, in Jacob's words at the end of the story: "I have seen God face to face, and yet my life is preserved."[16] This suggests that Jacob experienced the struggle as life-threatening: "a man" suddenly attacked him and tried to kill him, and in the end this "man" turns out to be God. The implications of this, however, only become clear in the larger context of the patriarchal narrative in Genesis. Luther's hermeneutic of this narrative is thoroughly Pauline; he has learned from the Apostle that the central issue in these stories is *the promise made to Abraham*, which is in substance the gospel, the promise of a coming descendent of Abraham in whom the nations will be blessed. The patriarchal stories are thus stories about what it means to live by a promise which has not yet been fulfilled, whose fulfillment indeed seems threatened at every turn.

As the son who has received the blessing from his father, Jacob's central role in the story is that of promise-bearer. He has to return to the land of Canaan and take possession of it, as Abraham did, so that his children may live in the land

---

15. *LW* 6:134.

16. *LW* 6:131-132, 136.

of promise. God has said to him: "Return to your country and to your kindred, and I will do you good" (Genesis 32:9).[17] His death would therefore be more than a private catastrophe; it would invalidate the promise of God.

It is significant then that Luther refers to the story of the binding of Isaac in his reflections on Jacob's distress of heart. "For Abraham, too, undoubtedly felt great trepidation and consternation in his whole person when he was commanded to kill his son."[18] Luther is reading that story in concert with the New Testament Letter to the Hebrews, for which the issue at stake is the promise that Isaac will be the son through whom Abraham has descendants.[19] Abraham's faith is ultimately faith in the resurrection: even if Isaac dies, he will still be the one from whom the line of Abraham extends into the future. "He considered that God was able to raise people even from the dead; hence, figuratively speaking, he did receive [Isaac] back" (Hebrews 11:19; alt.). Luther intimates that Jacob's persistence in wrestling with his attacker until the break of day displayed the same faith; he represents Jacob as saying, "No! No! ... God has given me orders, called me, and sent me to return to my fatherland; I shall not believe you or agree with you. Even though God kills me, well, let Him kill me, but I shall still live."[20]

What Luther is doing is not so much "psychologizing" the text as employing a vivid rhetorical strategy for bringing into focus what he believes are the deep theological and spiritual issues in the text. Here again, however, his sense of what "the text" is depends on his conviction that the Bible is a unified work with an intricate inner structure that bears witness to Christ. The Pauline linkage between "promise" and "gospel" is one way in which that unity and Christological

---

17. Cf. *LW* 6:109-111.

18. *LW* 6:132.

19.[Cf. *LW* 4:96: "...Abraham's trial was ... the contradiction of the promise."

20. *LW* 6:135.

focus can be discerned. The promise of Christ is the inner meaning of the promise of "seed" to Abraham.

But it would be fair to say that for Luther, as for the Church Fathers, there is no *single* interpretive strategy that suffices to bring out the gospel significance of the Old Testament. Thus in Genesis 32, we have seen Luther connecting the promise with the gospel by way of a Pauline strategy, and identifying the wrestler with Christ by way of a Johannine strategy. The Christ-attesting witness of Scripture is manifold and rich; it is there to be *discovered*, again and again, in ever-new ways, by the attentive and theologically aware reader.

3. Reading as Formation

A third aspect of Luther's dealing with Scripture demands our notice. When I was younger, I often found myself impatient with Luther's long exegetical discussions. I was looking for the theological pay-off and often found myself skimming my way through and cherry-picking the "good parts." My attitude changed, however, after some years of studying patristic and medieval-monastic exegesis. Traditional exegetes were not simply seeking to extract a "meaning" from the text, as though exegesis were like shelling peas, stripping away the textual hull to get at the discrete historical or doctrinal nuggets within.[21] Exegesis in the tradition was more like eating snow peas: the pod and the seeds are both nutritious, and must be consumed together, and are best chewed slowly and appreciatively. Engagement with the scriptural text is not preparation for the meal, like shelling peas; it *is* the meal. The nutrition is not separable from the verbal artifact of the text. Nor is all this merely a strange metaphor of mine: the image of "rumination," chewing the text like a cow chews its cud, was very common particularly in the monastic tradition.

---

21. For a discussion and critique of this model of interpretation, cf. Peter Leithart, *Deep Exegesis: The Mystery of Reading Scripture* (Waco: Baylor University Press, 2009), 1-24.

In a luminous recent study, Paul R. Kolbet has shown that for St. Augustine the engagement with the words of the Bible is itself a spiritual path. Learning to read the "signs" or words with reference to the realities of which they speak challenges our assumptions and exposes the corruptions of vision and desire with which we habitually engage the world. Kolbet describes Augustine's hermeneutic in this way:

> ...those who hear or read scripture encounter it assuming that they understand the world, yet they then find the text impossible to understand, since it does not conform to their customary habits of interpreting signs. They find that they cannot account for the gaps they perceive in scripture by their own constructions – that is, not merely their private, individual preferences, but the larger hermeneutical frameworks they inhabit and to which they appeal when trying to make sense of their experience. This then leads toward an aporetic state as the text whittles away the confidence of the reader to interpret signs. [Our habitual understanding of the world] gradually begins to lose its force as one discovers that it is what has been preventing understanding of the inspired text. As those reading persevere, they begin developing new habits of reference that increase their understanding of scripture and influence their judgments of value in the world.[22]

With very little, mostly terminological, change, this could be a description of Luther's interpretive assumptions as well. As for Augustine and monastic exegetes such as Bernard of Clairvaux, for Luther we do not read Scripture only to extract something from it. The reading itself changes us. When we take up a story like that of Jacob, Luther believes, we find

---

22. Paul R. Kolbet, *Augustine and the Cure of Souls: Revising a Classical Ideal* (Notre Dame, Indiana: University of Notre Dame Press, 2010), 150. This is Kolbet's summary of the hermeneutics of Augustine's *De doctrina christiana*.

it hard to understand because our own vision and affections are distorted. The difficulty is not just literary or linguistic; it is moral and spiritual. We are, for example, inclined to interpret struggle and conflict, the apparent contradiction of our faith and hope, as abandonment by God. Our "customary habit," in Kolbet's words, is to take tribulation and anxiety as "signs" that our trust in God has been in vain.

The story of Jacob walks us through this experience and overturns our assumptions. Tribulation ambushes Jacob in the form of a strong man who gives every appearance of wanting to kill him. Jacob is tempted to interpret this as a "sign" that God has abandoned him, that the blessing and promise of God have been revoked.[23] But Jacob does not give in or give up. Trust in the promise, though weakened and wavering, nonetheless persists in wrestling till the break of day.

Having persisted, Jacob comes in the end to see the situation quite differently: God wrestled with him, "not to destroy him but to confirm and strengthen him and that in this fight he might more correctly learn the might of the promise."[24] Jacob indeed *overcomes* God's testing by his faith in the promise; he has contended with God and prevailed. Along with Jacob, we begin to learn a new way of interpreting the signs of anguish and tribulation, both in the biblical story and in our own lives – because, for Luther, we *do* in fact live within the biblical story.

This not only applies to the high spiritual issues at stake in this example. Luther reads less dramatic details of the story in the same way. In Genesis 32:22, we are told that Jacob crossed the Jabbok in the middle of the night "with his two

---

23. "For although Jacob does not know who this man is, he nevertheless feels that he has been forsaken by God or that God is opposed to him and angry with him." *LW* 6:134.

24. *LW* 6:144.

wives, his two maids, and his eleven children," apparently, Luther writes, because "he was afraid that if his brother came in the morning, he would hinder his crossing."[25] But why does the word of God contain this apparently trivial information about Jacob's arrangements for his household? What would we lose if the text went straight to the wrestling-match and left this out?

For Luther, these domestic trivialities in the Genesis narrative constitute an important locus of spiritual formation. "We see… with what great care Moses, or rather, the Holy Spirit, describes even the most trifling actions and passions of the patriarchs, among which none of the showy and prodigious works such as the monks and the self-righteous boast of are prominent."

> But these passions are especially outstanding and golden because they have this promise, that not only their death and their blood are precious in the sight of the Lord (Ps. 116:15), but that even the hairs of their head are precious and numbered (Matt. 10:30). Therefore the Holy Spirit did not deem it unworthy to linger over these domestic and pastoral works and passions. For faith is exercised very well in these matters, and there ensues a sacrifice well-pleasing to God.[26]

Here again our perceptions of the world are being scrambled and rearranged as we struggle to make sense of Scripture. When we come to the Bible expecting a spiritually significant text, we find much in it that seems puzzling, unedifying, and unspiritual. Why are we reading so much about Jacob's household and even his livestock?

Luther believes that in just this dissonance between our assumptions about what is spiritual and edifying, on the one

---

25. *LW* 6:122.
26. *LW* 6:123.

hand, and the actual biblical narrative, on the other, we are being taught what everyday domestic and economic life *means to God.* Our habitual perception that such matters are trivial and unspiritual prevents us from understanding the Bible and therefore our own lives. Grasping why the Holy Spirit lingers over these details involves learning to see everyday life itself in a new way, as an arena of divine worship. Jacob making arrangements for his family and his goats and camels is in reality a priest making sacrifice to God. Because his actions are rooted in faith in God's promise and obedient to God's command, even his most trivial works and concerns are precious in God's sight. Thus by persevering with the Scriptures, we develop what Kolbet calls "new habits of reference," that is, we learn to read our own lives in a new light.

Conclusion

One of the great deficits in nineteenth- and twentieth-century Luther-research was its insufficient grasp of the scriptural character of his thinking – this despite many useful detailed studies of his biblical interpretation. The pea-shelling model tended to dominate; *understanding* Luther meant extracting doctrinal formulae or existential paradigms from his writing, leaving behind the biblical texts on which he was commenting. I would suggest that this leads easily to immense misunderstanding.

Let me take as an example the notorious formula *simul peccator et justus,* Luther's description of the Christian believer as "a sinner and a righteous person at the same time." It makes a great deal of difference that one of Luther's chief discussions of this slogan is found in his 1535 exegesis of Galatians 5:16.

Paul has been talking about love as the fulfillment of the law (v. 14) but also the continuing danger that believers will "bite and devour one another" (v. 15). The problem, Luther thinks, is that the reader might conclude from those verses that we must either justify ourselves by perfect love or else be damned. V. 16 is the Apostle's rejection of these alternatives: "But I say, walk by the Spirit and do not gratify the desires of the flesh."

It is in analyzing the theological underpinnings of this verse that Luther introduces *simul peccator et justus*. The believer does not love perfectly, but still experiences the desires of the flesh — the believer is still *peccator*. Yet at the same time, the believer has received the Spirit through faith in Christ, and therefore is not doomed to "gratify" those desires — the believer is at the same time a righteous person. The Spirit and the flesh have contrary desires, and struggle with one another, and in this struggle the believer is empowered to take sides with the Spirit: "if you are led by the Spirit you are not under the law," that is, not under condemnation, despite the continuing presence of disordered desire within. The *simul* describes the situation of the believer amidst this conflict of the Spirit and the flesh, by no means perfected yet justified by faith.

The point is that the slogan "sinner and righteous at the same time" does not float in the air, or stand by itself as an axiom from which conclusions can be deduced. It describes something going on in the scriptural text; its meaning is dependent on the texts which it illumines. The contemporary vulgar-Lutheran antinomian reading of the slogan, which makes it a kind of license to kill for believers, an assurance that there are no consequences for any amount of evil-doing so long as we "believe," could never have gained traction if it had not been abstracted from the formative process of reading in which it appears. For Luther, we learn what it *means* to be *simul peccator et justus* by pondering and ruminating texts like Galatians 5:16. It means to be caught up in a protracted conflict between our own disordered desire and the impulses of the Spirit; it does not mean living content with the flesh under the cover of "faith."

However, there is more at stake here than the possibility of better understanding Luther. Even more important is the prospect of learning from Luther to better understand Scripture. Listening to Luther wrestle like Jacob with biblical texts perhaps we can learn to see Scripture as Luther saw it, so that it might be for us what it was to him.

We will never understand Luther unless we realize that in all his work, he comes to us with an invitation to dwell with him in a particular textually-rendered reality, what Karl Barth famously called the "strange new world inside the Bible." If in our reading of Luther we are not carried with him into that world, if our engagement with Luther is not continually turning into a new engagement with the Bible, then we have taken hold of him the wrong way around. We will certainly not be learning what he most wanted to teach.

To be sure, Luther is not a perfect guide to the scriptural world; if we learn from him, it will have to mean learning also from his mistakes, some of which were whoppers. For example, Luther's apocalyptic demonization of Jews and the pope can be criticized from within the tradition as an exegetical mistake. He has not attended sufficiently to Ephesians 6:12: "We are not contending with flesh and blood, but against the principalities, against the powers, against the world rulers of this present darkness, against the spiritual hosts of wickedness in the heavenly places." From Origen at the latest onwards, this was read as a hermeneutical rule for understanding the phenomenon of "enemies" in Scripture, thus nudging the tradition away from preoccupation with flesh-and-blood opponents. This is a point on which Luther could have taken a lesson from Origen, who was not his favorite among the Fathers.

For those who do find themselves responding to his invitation, however, Luther is, with all his faults, one of the master explorers of Scripture; perhaps only Origen and Augustine are in his league. Like Augustine he did not find only "religion" in the Bible; he found the whole of human life there, from the political machinations of the powerful down to the trivial exasperations and weariness of everyday experience, re-described and reinterpreted within a world-embracing narrative whose center is the mystery of Christ. Like Augustine and Bernard of Clairvaux, he is astonishingly good at exposing the distorted perceptions and affections that hinder our understanding of the Bible and our inhabitation of its world. Furthermore, he is not only a teacher of Holy Scripture but a teacher of teachers; in his lectures, especially, he not only reads Scripture for his students but instructs them in the art of reading. Thus Luther not only offers us his own readings of the Bible but invites us to go on in the same way. For one of Luther's most fervent beliefs about Scripture was that the Bible is *inexhaustible*:

> Therefore let us shake off ... self-flattery and humble ourselves before the Holy Spirit, and let us confess that this is an infinite wisdom, which could not be exhausted were we to spend our whole lives in learning the Scriptures.... For something always shines forth which before was hidden from us; something always delights which before we passed over as uninteresting.[27]

---

27. Luther, "Preface" to his published lectures on the Psalms of Degrees, *WA* 40/III, 11.

The Scripture Controversy in American Lutheranism:

Infallibility, Inerrancy, Inspiration

Mark A. Granquist

Perhaps it is true, what they say: "The more important something is to you, the more you tend to fight about it." Most Lutherans, indeed most Christians, hold that the Word of God, the canonical Scriptures of the Old and New Testaments, is the key way of hearing the true, revelatory voice of God, and have held that these Scriptures are the norm and rule of their understanding of God, of Christ, and of life together in the Christian Church. For something that is of such importance, then, it should not be surprising that Lutheran Christians in America have continually wrestled with and even fought over the nature of Scripture and its authority in their lives and communities. The history of American Lutherans in the twentieth century can be written in terms of the controversies over Scripture, which have seriously engaged their churches and denominations. The question is thus not whether they will continue to wrestle with these issues; the question is, instead, whether their struggles will result in a deeper and more fruitful understanding of the nature and authority of Scripture, or whether these discussions become so divisive and bitter that they cannot learn from each other, and simply retreat into polarized, absolutistic bunkers. Confidence in the authority of the Word of God is one thing; confidence in the absolute certainty of our own theological positions is certainly something else.

To understand these controversies and the impact they have had on the present and future of American Lutheranism, it is important to think about the historical contexts of these twentieth-century American Lutheran controversies. Of course, it is important to look back briefly at Martin Luther and later Lutheran theologians, as well as the normative documents in the Lutheran *Book of Concord*. But it will also be equally important to look at the modern and North American contexts behind these controversies, especially the Enlightenment, the rise of Liberalism, the challenge of modernity and science, as well as the immediate context; an immigrant, hybridized Lutheranism in America coming of age and learning to "do" Lutheranism in English, in an American context dominated by Reformed or Calvinist Protestantism.

As is usual with Lutherans, the argument goes back to Martin Luther himself, and as is all too common with Lutherans, Luther himself seems not to settle the argument definitively. Rather, in Luther's voluminous writings there does seem to be copious ammunition for those with differing understandings of the nature of biblical authority. Some claim Luther as an advocate of infallibility and inerrancy, while others find in his works a position rather apart from these terms. So Luther could claim a very high view of scriptural authority, yet in a number of instances he was also critical and even dismissive of sections of the biblical canon, and seemed to value some biblical passages as more central than others. But, far from being two-minded about Scripture, Luther valued it very highly as the means by which believers encountered the salvific Word of God; his dialectical theology resisted any forms of reductionism, and this is very true about his understanding of Scripture. Equally, the Lutheran confessional documents value the authority of Scripture very highly, referring to Scripture as the supreme norm (*norma normans*) which judges all other forms of theological authority (*norma normata*). Yet the Confessions do not always help directly in the modern argument; their focus, as it was for Luther, is on the conflict between different types of religious authority. They hold Scripture as the highest authority concerning the Word of God, higher than tradition or individual judgment. Beyond this, they do not go into specifics.

Ever interested in absolutely nailing down theological argument to the smallest detail, the seventeenth-century Lutheran Orthodox theologians attempted to "clean up" Lutheran understandings of biblical authority by precisely defining the nature of biblical authority, and they did so by using the terms "inerrancy" and "infallibility," the first time these terms appear in Lutheranism. Their general movement towards a static, objectivized statement of Christian theology was opposed by a succeeding generation of Lutheran theologians, the Pietists, who sought the authority of Scripture more in the subjective and emotional reactions of the believer to the proclamation of the Word of God; for them, the Word of God worked through the Holy Spirit to transform lives and communities. But in their attempt to save the "living" Word of God active in the believer and in the world, the Pietists unwittingly opened the door to Enlightenment liberals, such as Schleiermacher. These liberals understood the norming norm to reside within the rational individual, and thus the educated, enlightened person could read Scripture and determine, individually, the truth or falsity of the Scriptures themselves.

Among nineteenth-century European Lutherans, two different schools of Lutheran confessional theology attempted to stem the tide of rationalism and liberalism. Repristination theology looked back to the seventeenth-century scholastic Orthodox theologians, and adopted the same terminology, namely, inerrancy and infallibility, to define the Lutheran understanding of biblical authority. The somewhat less conservative Erlangen school saw biblical authority in more dynamic terms, avoiding the terms "inerrant" and "infallible"; these theologians understood the Word of God working dynamically in history, the revelation of God which "called, enlightened, and sanctified" the community of faith, the church. In this understanding, Scripture needed to be understood as a complete whole, rather than as individual points of doctrine. Both of these nineteenth-century schools of Lutheran theology had an important impact on American Lutheranism in the twentieth century.

As important as these European Lutheran developments were, however, the context of American Christianity, predominantly Calvinist Protestant in nature, was perhaps even more important. From its beginnings, Calvinism has had a more robust and strictly defined doctrine of scriptural authority than did Lutheranism; this has historically been one of the distinctive elements of the Reformed tradition. It was this Reformed Protestant tradition that was crucial in developing the traditional understanding of the American state as the "redeemer nation," which brought with it a major moral push to institute biblical morality (as they saw it) into the civil and political life of the United States. Also, it was this Calvinist tradition that began the battle against scientific modernism in the late nineteenth century, dividing the liberal Protestants, who believed they could co-opt the new science, from the conservatives, who saw this new modernism as antithetical to their entire religious enterprise. The older, Enlightenment liberalism of the eighteenth century was essentially Deistic, believing in a Creator God and a natural moral law; this fit uncomfortably with traditional Protestant Christianity, but there were points of contact (especially moralism) which they could agree. But the new, nineteenth-century scientific modernism was different; it believed in no absolutes beyond the scientific process itself, and came to believe that traditional religious beliefs about Scripture, and even God, were not scientifically valid. This nineteenth-century challenge to traditional religion would threaten to replace religion with secular forms of "salvation," namely, the betterment of the world and humanity through scientific progress.

American religious leaders (mainly Reformed Protestants) became intensely divided over this new challenge. Those who were moving toward theological liberalism believed that there was much in the old, static Christian theology that was outdated and no longer useful; in fact, maintaining such doctrines, such as the inerrancy of Scripture, was harmful to Christianity. To reconcile Christianity with the new scientific world-view, Christianity had to jettison the outdated parts of the traditional scriptural world-view; doing so would illuminate the eternal "core" of Scripture, and in so doing make Christianity relevant again for modern, "scientific" people. On the other hand, the conservatives reacted to the challenge of scientific modernity by "circling the wagons"; in their minds, science was the enemy, an alien world-view that had to be repulsed at the outer gates of Christianity. If one gave in to the new world-view at any particular point, the defensive walls would be breached, and the whole of Christianity would be threatened with loss. Absolute biblical authority had to be maintained at all costs, and the use of terms such as inerrant and infallible to define it became widespread. The metaphors of warfare are apt here; many Christians saw this threat from scientific modernism in starkly apocalyptic terms. Modernity was the incarnation of the Anti-Christ, and this was a holy war to maintain true Christian faith.

Proponents of Liberalism and Conservatism battled each other intensely for control of Protestant denominations and institutions from the 1890s through the 1920s. The conservatives lost this "Fundamentalist-Modernist" controversy, and split off from the Mainline Protestant denominations, which was the beginning of the division of American Protestantism into separate Mainline and Evangelical streams, a division which continues to this day. It was this battle, and the ways in which each position on biblical authority were defined, that formed the backdrop against which American Lutherans struggled to define their own distinctive understanding of biblical authority in the twentieth century.

American Lutherans were certainly influenced by this controversy raging about them, the controversy over definitions of scriptural authority. Lutherans did not fit easily into one camp or another. Lutherans also did not work naturally with the definitions of scriptural authority that were common in the larger controversy. The categories and terminology of the Fundamentalist-Modernist controversy were essentially Calvinist at their root, and reflected Reformed Protestant assumptions about the Bible. Calvinism traditionally had assumed a very close correlation between the Word of God and the written Scriptures, which had, over the centuries, deeply shaped their forms of worship and church life. Only those elements which came directly out of the text of Scripture could be used in their congregations, which is why, for example, that their hymnody was limited to Psalms and biblical paraphrases. Even when American Evangelicals in the nineteenth century moved away from Calvinism towards Arminianism, their attitude towards Scripture remained essentially unchanged. Given this attitude, the Bible was taken as the absolute guide to all elements of life.

Lutheran understandings of Scripture were different. For Lutherans, the category of "Gospel" could mean anything which proclaimed the truth about the saving power of Jesus Christ; in Luther's words, what "pushed" Christ. For Lutherans, the primary source of this proclamation of Christ was Christ himself, in his incarnation, death, and resurrection. The books of the Bible were the chief record and norm of this proclamation, but a good sermon, one that "pushed Christ," could also be in this sense the Word of God. On the other hand, there were parts of the Scripture that, although important, did not emphasize the gospel message so much; hence Luther's famous saying that the Epistle of James was an "epistle of straw." Those elements of the Bible that really didn't have quite so much to do with proclamation were, in this sense then, of less direct impact. The Scriptures then are the key to an understanding of the Word of God, but not everything in Scripture was of equal weight or importance.

At the turn of the twentieth century most American Lutherans were still relative newcomers to America. Though the colonial Lutherans in the Muhlenberg tradition had been in America for hundreds of years, and had already transitioned to the use of English, the bulk of Lutherans in the Midwest did not undergo this transition until after the First World War. Lutheran theology had not seriously been done in the English language before, and American Lutherans had their hands full simply keeping up with the millions of new European immigrants. Theological writings and conflicts among American Lutherans in the nineteenth century were focused almost exclusively on questions of confessional authority; Lutherans generally agreed among themselves that the Scripture was their doctrinal rule and norm, and didn't really worry too much about the issue.[1]

In the early twentieth century there were virtually no American Lutherans that could be considered liberals or modernists. Unlike some European Lutherans, the dominant forms of Lutheranism in the United States came out of the evangelical and confessional awakenings of the nineteenth century, and American Lutherans were generally dismayed by the forms of liberal theology and biblical criticism that were present in some European Lutheran universities. Liberalism, whether in its European or American forms, hardly existed among the American Lutheran denominations, which

---

1. For an overview about American Lutherans and the question of scriptural authority, see E. Clifford Nelson, ed., *The Lutherans in North America.* Philadelphia: Fortress Press, 1975, especially pages 384-85, 409-10, 443-46, and 458-68.

were generally conservative, with various grades of such conservatism. But though they were conservative, they were also generally not the kind of conservatism that defined American evangelicals and fundamentalists. These American Lutheran conservatives believed deeply in the authority of the Bible, but did not conceptualize that authority along the dominant Calvinistic lines. American Lutherans were worried about the new scientific modernism that was rolling through sectors of the United States, but did not reject modernity along the lines of American Fundamentalism. For example, during the evolution controversies of the 1920s the vast majority of Lutherans rejected evolution, but generally did not join the Fundamentalist crusade to pass laws forbidding the teaching of evolution. To most American Lutherans, evolution was not a direct and serious threat to the gospel proclamation about Christ and his benefits. It was most certainly wrong, they were sure of this, but they were not too worried about its inroads into their faith communities.

Nevertheless, they were sufficiently worried about scientific modernism that when they began to do Lutheran theology in English, in the early twentieth century, they wanted to make sure that their proclamations were sufficiently conservative. For some American Lutherans, their concern led them to adopt new English theological words that seemed to state what they believed about Scripture, namely, the declaration of scriptural authority using the terms "inerrant" and "infallible." These were terms that did have some history and currency among Lutherans from the seventeenth century onward, but terms that were generally not used in the same fashion and with the same meaning as when used by American Fundamentalists. It is very difficult to trace the shades of nuance meant by these early twentieth-century American Lutherans. The key question is this: by using these terms, did they consciously mean to adopt an essentially Reformed understanding of Scripture, or were they trying to make the

English terms "inerrant" and "infallible" fit their Lutheran theological understanding of Scripture? Most likely they did initially intend to use "inerrant" and "infallible" to define a traditional Lutheran doctrine of Scripture, although as the century moved along, some groups did move toward a more American Evangelical understanding, whether consciously or unconsciously, it is difficult to tell.

As the various Lutheran denominations moved toward cooperation and union with each other, the technical terms they used in English surrounding the authority of Scripture grew more contentious, especially the words inerrant, infallible, and inspired. In the Norwegian union of 1917, for example, the constitution only stated that the Scriptures were

> the revealed Word of God, and therefore the only source and rule of faith, doctrine, and life.[2]

In the ULCA merger of 1918, this constitution states that the Scriptures were the

> inspired Word of God, and as the only infallible rule and standard of faith and practice.[3]

But controversies arose in the 1920s, both with the formation of a cooperative organization, the National Lutheran Council, and with the merger of the Ohio, Iowa, and Buffalo Synods to constitute the "old" American Lutheran Church in 1930.

The National Lutheran Council was founded in 1918 to be a cooperative organization among different Lutheran denominations, its powers and duties carefully limited to "ex-

---

2. "Constitution of the Norwegian Lutheran Church in America, chapter 1, section 2 (1917)," in *The Union Documents of the Evangelical Lutheran Church.* Minneapolis: Evangelical Lutheran Church, 1948, p. 75.

3. "The Constitution of the United Lutheran Church in America, article II, section 1 (1918)," in Richard C. Wolf, ed., *Documents of Lutheran Unity in America.* Philadelphia: Fortress Press, 1966, p. 273.

ternal" matters, and not implying unity of doctrine. But of course in practice it was (as leaders of the Missouri Synod pointedly noted) almost impossible to limit matters to externals only. A year later, President H.G. Stub of the Norwegian Lutheran Church in America introduced a set of theological theses (the Chicago Theses) that he hoped the NLC would adopt. In terms of Scripture, Stub took the NLCA constitution wording, but added the word "inerrant" to the phrase. It read, Scripture is:

> the inspired and inerrant Word of God, and therefore the only source and rule of faith, doctrine, and life.[4]

But other members of the Council, especially from the ULCA, did not agree with this. Modified in 1925 at Minneapolis, the Chicago-Minneapolis Theses became a document attempting to unite the Midwestern conservatives, but not a pan-Lutheran statement.

Among the Midwestern Lutheran Synods that formed the "old" American Lutheran Church in 1930 (the Ohio, Iowa, Buffalo, and Texas Synods), a controversy over the term "inerrant" arose unexpectedly during their negotiations, when it became apparent that although they agreed on the use of the word "inerrant," they did not agree on what the term meant, and how it applied to an understanding of biblical authority. In 1926, the committee charged with the ALC constitution proposed language about Scripture that mirrored the Chicago-Minneapolis theses, including the phrase "inspired and inerrant Word of God." The delegates of the Iowa Synod objected and proposed an alternative reading, stating that the Scriptures were

> the inspired Word of God and the only inerrant source, norm, and guide of faith and life.[5]

---

4. "The Chicago Theses, preamble (1919)," in Wolf, *Documents*, p. 298.

5. "Iowa Revision of Doctrinal Statement (1926)," in Wolf, *Documents*, p. 331.

A major controversy erupted, as it seemed to the others that Iowa was apparently "soft" on scriptural authority. In 1928, the Iowa Synod clarified its position on the authority of Scripture:

> When we confess the inerrancy of the Bible, as we now have it, we do not maintain that there are no inaccuracies of transcription, different readings, omissions, and minor additions to the original text, or that there are no passages which *to us* seem to be contradictions or discrepancies, which, however, do not affect the interests of salvation or faith.[6]

Remarkably, this explanation managed to assuage the fears of the other partners, and when the ALC was formed in 1930, its constitution referred to Scripture as the "inspired Word of God and the only infallible authority."[7] The word "inerrant" was not used.

This controversy illuminates a key uncertainty among Lutherans at the time, namely, what the term "inerrant" meant, and what areas of Scripture did this inerrancy cover? Did it mean that every line and word of Scripture was inerrant, or only that Scripture was inerrant when it referred to, as Iowa stated, "the interests of salvation and faith?" Was there perhaps a Lutheran understanding of inerrancy that suggested the possibility of factual errors in the Bible, but that such possible errors did not affect the theological reliability of the Scriptures? If this is its position, then, was the word "inerrant" really proper to use at this point?

Perhaps with these ambiguities in mind the Missouri Synod developed its own statement of faith, the "Brief Statement" of 1932, which is still one of the main statements of

---

6. "Report of the Thirty-Fifth General Convention of the Evangelical Lutheran Synod of Iowa and Other States," Chicago: n.p., 1928, p. 149.

7. "Constitution of the American Lutheran Church, article II, section 1 (1930)," in Wolf, *Documents*, p. 145.

the theological position of the Synod. In this statement, syn-odical drafters avoided the word "inerrant," though in much greater detail they insisted on the absolute reliability of the biblical text in every instance, theological or otherwise. The statement referred to the "inspiration" of Scripture, its "ver-bal inspiration," and then concluded

> it goes without saying that (the Scriptures) contain no errors or contradictions, but that they are in all their parts and words the infallible truth, also in those parts which treat of historical, geographical, and other secular matters....[8]

Without using the perhaps imprecise word "inerrant," the Missouri Synod made its position even clearer, coming much closer to the position of conservative American Evangelical-ism than the other Lutheran denominations.

The Lutheran contention over inerrancy continued through the middle of the twentieth century. In 1944 Johan Michel Reu of the Iowa Synod published a book on Luther and the Scriptures, in which he claimed that Luther held the Bible errorless, even in secular matters, perhaps moving more closely to the Missouri Synod's position.[9] In 1948, ULCA theologian Joseph Sittler published his lectures on the con-cept of the "Word of God," which argued for limiting the authority of Scripture to its theological and religious validity, and suggested that the move toward a more strict "dictation theory" by seventeenth-century Lutheran dogmaticians was a "caricature" of Luther's own position.[10] When the "new" American Lutheran Church was formed in 1960, its consti-

---

8. "Of the Holy Scriptures," *Brief Statement of the Doctrinal Position of the Missouri Synod*. St. Louis: Concordia Publishing House, 1932.

9. J. Michael Reu, *Luther and the Scriptures*. Columbus, OH: The Wartburg Press, 1944.

10. Joseph Sittler, *The Doctrine of the Word in the Structure of Lutheran Theology*. Philadelphia: Muhlenberg Press, 1948.

tution employed the term "inerrant" to describe Scripture

> ...in all their parts as the divinely inspired, revealed, and inerrant Word of God...."[11]

But the inclusion of this inerrancy language in the ALC constitution was uncomfortable for a number of ALC leaders and theologians, who subsequently attempted to blunt the original intention of the language by suggesting that the term "inerrant" modified the "Word of God" and not the "Bible." Lutheran historian E. Clifford Nelson suggested of the ALC constitution that

> its Fundamentalistic language proved to be an embarrassment and provoked church leaders to make "interpretations" which were not in accord with the historical circumstances and intentions out of which the statement grew....[12]

The constitution of the Lutheran Church in America, formed two years later, made no mention of the term "inerrant," stating that Scripture was the "norm for faith and life" and "divinely inspired record of God's redemptive act in Christ...."[13] When the LCA and ALC merged in 1988 to form the Evangelical Lutheran Church in America, the term "inerrant" was not used. It was fairly clear that since the Second World War, ALC and LCA seminaries and colleges were increasingly comfortable with the use of higher biblical criticism in their teaching of the Scriptures, although they still would maintain the Scriptures as in some sense the inspired Word of God.

---

11. "Constitution of the American Lutheran Church, article IV, section 1 (1960)," in Wolf, *Documents*, pp. 523-33.

12. "Footnote 54," Nelson, *The Lutherans in North America*, p. 468. See also E. Clifford Nelson, *Lutheranism in North America, 1914-1970*. Minneapolis: Augsburg Publishing House, 1972, pp. 178-80.

13. "Constitution of the Lutheran Church in America, article II, section 3 (1962)," in Wolf, *Documents*, p. 566.

Within the Missouri Synod, despite the Brief Statement of 1932, there were some theologians and exegetes who were cautiously exploring a less restrictive position on Scripture. The great Missouri conflict of the 1960s and 1970s was directly tied to a dispute over the nature of biblical authority. The "examination" or "purge" of the Concordia Seminary Faculty was directly related to this topic. With the departure of the "Moderate" wing of the LCMS into the AELC and then the ELCA, the lines between the two positions were acutely drawn.

So far, then, the historical sketch of this issue. What then might be said about this subject in contemporary American Lutheranism? Some ideas and suggestions.

First, it is fairly clear that American Lutherans were drawn into controversy over the authority of Scripture in large measure due to the influence of the battle that raged (and still rages) among other American Protestants, especially those in the Reformed and Evangelical traditions. The American Lutheran formulations of biblical authority tend to reflect positions within this alien dispute. American Lutherans have never completely divorced themselves from this external dispute, and have never really settled the issue of biblical authority by means of Luther himself and the Lutheran confessional tradition.

Second, the words "infallible" and "inerrant," by themselves, are of rather limited value. We have seen how these words were interpreted by different American Lutheran authors and denominations with different meanings and understandings, creating at times more heat than light. These words, too, have not really been all that useful and helpful in restraining the possible "erosion" of biblical authority in Lutheran denominations. The "new" ALC had the words "inerrant" and "infallible" in its constitution from 1960 to 1988, but the presence of those words, by themselves, did virtually nothing to dispel the widespread adoption of higher biblical criticism within that denomination. A strong declaration of biblical authority in the Missouri Synod did nothing to curb conflict over the issue.

Third, those American Lutherans who resist terms such as "inerrant" and "infallible" have generally resisted any substantial discussions involving the nature of scriptural authority at all. It seems that, in wishing not to be seen as Fundamentalists, they have bent over backwards to avoid anything approaching normative statements about Scripture, or much of anything that would curb the human position as arbiter over scriptural content and authority. Many of the more "liberal" American Lutherans seem to have unlimited confidence in human abilities to judge Scripture, and little sense that Scripture should be normative over the human person.

Fourth, in the ELCA at least, it seems that there is a larger question than simply the nature of scriptural authority; rather the question is whether there is any outside normative authority that can check or rein in human judgments. In the recent controversy about gay pastors, it seemed that proponents of allowing such a change were reduced to suggesting that the Bible simply had little or no relevance to the debate at all. When confronted by passages that would seem to uphold traditional morality, proponents of the change often said that such passages were simply irrelevant, that the context of those passages in the Bible only reflected a situation that no longer existed, and that the Bible just did not envision the contemporary situation. Many lay people, swayed by emotional appeals, simply agreed that the Bible was no check on what human feelings and emotions conceptualized as the truth. In such a situation, conceptions of scriptural authority simply lost all relevance; Scripture was important only insofar as it confirms one's own human judgments. It is perhaps time that the theological struggle concentrate more on a redefinition of the human person, one that attacked this pervasive optimism that the human person's judgments are ultimately authoritative.

Fifth, both sides of the issue on scriptural authority have seemingly lost any sense of the traditional Lutheran deference to scriptural authority, and especially the traditional Lutheran position that one uses Scripture to define Scripture – the sense of the large context and intercontextuality of biblical authority. Conservatives often resort to proof texting by quoting Bible passages at random, transgressing the Lutheran understanding of the Word of God as that which "pushes" Christ, and totally ignoring the implication of the Lutheran doctrine of Law and Gospel. Liberals, on the other hand, are often seemingly willing simply to dismiss or marginalize passages that they do not like, or that are inconvenient, without struggling over the larger biblical context of these passages, or how other passages of Scripture might illuminate the ones that are difficult to understand or to accept.

In a 2007 article in *Lutheran Quarterly*, biblical scholar Erik Heen addressed the questions of biblical interpretation in the contemporary world.[14] In this article, Heen quoted from the critique of "inerrancy" as a category for scriptural authority by Gerhard Forde. After an appreciation of the positive aspects of "inerrancy" to describe biblical authority, Forde then suggested the negative aspect of this term:

> ...if I say that there can't be any errors in Scripture if it is to be the Word of God, then I am in effect saying that I know what the Word of God must be, and unless Scripture meets my idea it cannot be accepted.

After suggesting that this puts human authority above God's authority, Forde continued:

> The fact is that I *do not know a priori* what the Word of God is. I don't know beforehand what God is

---

14. Erik Heen, "The Theological Interpretation of the Bible," *Lutheran Quarterly*, 21(4), Winter 2007, pp. 373-403.

going to say or how; I can listen, and then try to form some confession as to what it is after I have heard it.[15]

Although Forde is discussing the more conservative inerrantist side of this debate, the same critique also applies equally to the more liberal positions. These liberal positions on Scripture seem to end up saying in effect, "if there is something in the Bible that seems to run contrary to my own understanding or judgment, then my judgment must take precedent. If it seems unreasonable to me, then it is unreasonable." Both positions, in effect, dictate to God and to Scripture the ground rules under which a person might come to believe or accept scriptural authority. Both positions are, in effect, idolatry – putting oneself in the position of God.

As a biblical scholar who himself finds utility in higher biblical criticism, Heen eventually suggested that dialog between the Lutheran extremes on the question of scriptural authority might actually be beneficial. He says:

> It may, in fact be wisest not to speak for God in a definitive way concerning the use of Scripture in the church by taking a stand on the infallibility of Scripture. If this is accepted as a prudent theological judgment, then one might even see the robust expression of two quite different understandings of Scripture as a resource and not a deficit within the contemporary church. That is, *if* those who find themselves within the two hermeneutical trajectories find it possible to suspend judgment on the issue of inerrancy, *then* perhaps common ground can

---

15. Gerhard Forde, "Law and Gospel as the Methodological Principle of Theology" in *Theological Perspectives: A Discussion of Contemporary Issues in Lutheran Theology* (by members of the Department of Religion, Luther College), Decorah, IA: Luther College Press, 1964, quoted in Heen, "The Theological Interpretation of the Bible," p. 388-89.

be found with regard to Scripture's intended *efficacy* as a means of grace, which I would argue, is far more characteristic of historical Lutheran hermeneutics than the doctrine of inerrancy.[16]

This seems like a good judgment, though it would also be important to have all participants in such a dialog also agree that the Bible does indeed have a normative authority over the judgments of human persons and even the Church, even when such normative judgments seem to limit human freedom and expressions. Perhaps Lutherans need to humbly and submissively *listen* more to Scripture, and what it says to them. Perhaps this would be better than arguing about the terms under which they are willing to grant Scripture authority over themselves.

---

16. Heen, "The Theological Interpretation of the Bible," pp. 391-92.

Knowing the Bible through the Liturgy

The Holy Scripture as Doxology

Amy C. Schifrin, STS

> The Bible is in the liturgy as a fish in water.... Never
> does the Bible come as much into its own truth than
> when it is proclaimed in the ekklesia, the place where
> the liturgy lays out the constitutive dimensions of
> the Bible. We can thus speak of a sacramentality of
> the scriptures, a sacramentality which is not acci-
> dental to them, but quite essential.[1]
>
> – Louis-Marie Chauvet

St. Paul writes a benediction to the Corinthians, *The Grace
of our Lord Jesus Christ, the love of God and the fellowship of
the Holy Spirit be with you all* (2 Cor. 13:3), and it becomes
our greeting as the assembly gathers to give God thanks and
praise. In a village between Samaria and Galilee ten ragged
lepers cry out to Jesus of Nazareth, *Lord have mercy* (Luke
17:13), and through their voices we pray for the peace from
above and for our salvation. Angels sing glory over the Savior's
birth in Bethlehem and a cantor invites us to join in praise of
the Triune God, *Glory to God in the highest and peace to his people
on earth* (Luke 2:14). John on Patmos sees rocky soil beneath
his feet and the vast expanse of sea that separates him from
his beloved community and then he looks to the future in

---

1. Louis-Marie Chauvet, "What Makes the Liturgy Biblical?—Texts," *Studia
   Liturgica* 22 (1992): 127-128.

which God will unite the voices of the faithful in praise, *Blessing, Honor, Glory and Might be to God and the Lamb forever Amen. This is the feast of victory for our God* (Rev. 5:12-13;7:12). And then as Boaz meets the reapers in the field, his words, too, become ours as they prepare us to pray, *The Lord be with you* (Ruth 2:4).

Liturgy and Scripture are a unified whole: indissoluble and enduring, coming to the people of God through the breath of the Holy Spirit. For just as God took a handful of dust and breathed life into the man's nostrils and the man became a living being, and just as the Risen Christ came to the disciples and breathed peace into their fearful hearts and they believed, so now he breathes this same life-creating, reconciling breath into our lives, so that we, too, can respond with our neighbor, *And also with you*. From the event of creation to its remembrance in the Scriptures to its sounding in the Eucharistic liturgy, God, Father, Son, and Holy Spirit is at work bringing order out of chaos, strength out of weakness, hope out of suffering, forgiveness out of rebellion, and life out of death.

When the living Word of God, Jesus Christ, speaks, his words carry the same power that brought the universe to life. When his word is sounded in the assembly, that same power is released into our lives. That word was recorded in what we've come to know as the Canon of Scripture, the Holy Bible, but the way in which this written word came to be known to us was through the liturgy, through the public reading of the prophets and of the memoirs of the apostles in the context of a community gathered by the Holy Spirit for prayer, for praise, and most decidedly for Thanksgiving, that is, for The Great Thanksgiving, the Eucharist.[2] For here, when

---

2. "And on the day called Sunday, all who live in cities or in the country gather together to one place, and the memoirs of the apostles or the writings of the prophets are read, as long as time permits; then, when the reader has ceased, the president verbally instructs, and exhorts to the imitation of these good things. Then we all rise together and pray, and, as

bread is broken and wine is poured, all that Christ has done on our behalf is made mysteriously clear. God enters human history, and the act of worship becomes the place to tell that history and look ahead to where he will be leading us. What is told in the worshipping assembly, what bears witness to God's Holy History, comes to be known to us as Holy Scripture – the Bible.[3]

The topic before us, "Knowing the Bible through the Liturgy," is of vital importance to us as a church for we live in the tension between a world, on the one hand, that does not know God's Holy History or rejects his Holy History, so that people don't know how to live in the present or how to desire the future to which he points;[4] and on the other hand, a popular religious and cultural milieu that knows some of the words of Scripture but only knows them apart from the witness of the faithful community which has been created by receiving the Living Lord through the Preaching of the Word and the reception of the Holy Sacraments that provide the

---

we before said, when our prayer is ended, bread and wine and water are brought, and the president in like manner offers prayers and thanksgivings, according to his ability, and the people assent, saying Amen...." Justyn Martyr, *First Apology*, Chapter 67.

3. "The canonization of Scripture means that only these writings can be read in the church's liturgical assembly. This issue transcends any form critical analysis of the liturgical provenance of certain Biblical books or passages within them. The point is that the Bible emerged as Holy Scripture by canonizing the books that were read publicly in the synagogues of the Jews and the assemblies of Christians. It follows from this that the liturgy itself supplies the essential hermeneutical perspectives for the exegesis and application of Scripture." Frank Senn, "Liturgy and Dogma," *Lutheran Forum*, (Winter 1999): 22.

4. "The usual notion of inspiration obscures the Scriptural narrative. This is indeed a major flaw, for whenever the church has had a firm grasp of her own conviction, it has read the Scripture as one long narrative of the history of God with his people, of the coming of Christ and the kingdom." Robert Jenson, *On the Inspiration of Scripture* (Delhi, NY: ALPB, 2012), 48.

shape of the historic liturgy.[5] Between atheism on the one hand, which pretends to be enlightened, and an anti-sacramental Protestantism on the other, a brand of Protestantism in which the interpretation of that Holy History is privatized against a rigidly black and white backdrop, the world is still in dire need of experiencing the salvation that comes from the One God who calls into being that which did not exist.

Yet before we go too quickly to the Sunday gatherings on the Lord's Day, let us first go to the place where hearing by faith (Rom. 10:17) begins: The Order for Holy Baptism.

I. Holy Baptism

Out of the swirling waters God brought a world into being. Back into the deep he plunged a humanity whose sin was coursing like white-water rapids in their veins. A dove makes an entrance when the danger is passed (Gen. 8:11).

With a pillar of cloud by day and a pillar of fire by night, God led his people out of slavery into the freedom of the Promised Land. Through the water, wet and wild, they splashed their way to new life in his name. Miriam did the first liturgical dance and I'm sure her brothers took up the chorus (Ex. 15:2-21).

Joshua, Son of Nun, comes through the Jordan, heralding all that is come. These are but the first of many walls to come tumbling down (Josh. 6:5).

God tells us of his saving work through narrative and proclamatory language. This language is also highly symbolic, for it points beyond itself to what is to come. Even more, it

---

5. "Faithful interpretation of scripture requires a trinitarian hermeneutics. The rule of faith demands that scripture be read as a coherent dramatic narrative, the unity of which depends on its principal actor: the God who has forever known himself and who, in the history of redemption, has revealed himself to us, as the Father, the Son, and the Holy Spirit." Timothy George, *First Things*, no. 211 (Mr 2011): 30.

points to who is to come. The term that the church Fathers used for the people who inhabited God's Holy History from the birth of mankind was "figure" or "type." Moses was a figure of Jesus, and Joshua was as well. The eight people afloat in the midst of a deluge was a figure of the 8th day, the new creation, the day of resurrection (1 Peter 3:17-22). In these rich accounts that God has given us in the Old Testament, he is preparing us for the moment of his incarnation. As he gives us this highly symbolic, eschatological word, he is preparing us to receive Jesus Christ as Lord of all.

The Old Testament, that Word which tells the story of God's love from the dawning of creation until the fullness of the incarnation, is the setting in which we receive our Savior. What the church has understood as "figure" becomes "reality" in the conception, birth, ministry, suffering, death, resurrection, and ascension of Jesus her Lord.[6] When he is sheltered in his mother's womb, the world knows little of his presence. Yet his cousin John, still bathed in the amniotic waters of Elizabeth, will sense his growing presence, in anticipation of their wade in the Jordan to come (Luke 1:41). And it is that sojourn into the Jordan that points the way to our baptism into his death for our sake, and his resurrection, the victory of our God over all things.

Baptismal liturgies have undergone changes over the centuries, yet even as the rites evolve there remain some common elements: water and word, prayer and thanksgiving; renunciation and anointing; instruction and profession of faith, and even candles and clothing. The first Christians to be baptized were adults, yet Scripture gives evidence of whole households receiving this sacred sign (Acts 16:15; Acts 16:33-34; and 1 Cor. 1:16). Five centuries later, infant baptism was the norm in the West, but whether administered to a howling

---

6. See Jean Daniélou, S.J., *The Bible and the Liturgy* (Notre Dame, IN: University of Notre Dame Press, 1956), 70-113.

infant or to an adult whose last breaths are labored and slow, everything that the Holy Scriptures bear witness to in regard to God's love and mercy is given in its fullness on that day. However long we live in this world, we will be living out his righteousness, his innocence, his blessedness, for the promise of the One who made the universe in love is now ours.

We begin to know God's Holy History in the baptismal rite itself. We begin to know that we are part of his Holy History. As my friend Gordon Lathrop reminds us, "The liturgy is the Bible alive."[7] Since we have only an hour (not a semester) I want to have us look at just three elements in the *LBW* Baptismal Order:[8] The Thanksgiving over the water; the Baptism, i.e., the washing in the name of the Father, and of the Son, and of the Holy Spirit; and the prayer for the Holy Spirit. And then we will be ready to talk about Holy Communion, the Eucharist.

The Thanksgiving begins with a preface dialog, reminding the assembly in whose name and by whose Spirit they have been gathered. It moves to a posture of thanksgiving, for the One who will bring forth new life from these waters is the same One who has done so from the beginning of time. In using two of the same "sentences" in common with the Great Thanksgiving (*The Lord be with you...* and *Let us give thanks...*), a subtle yet ever-present connection is sounded, for those who are baptized will be renewed and strengthened at their Lord's Table throughout this life-long journey.[9] (As

---

7. "To people who know the biblical story, the very actions of the gathering may seem like the Bible alive." Gordon W. Lathrop, *Holy Things: A Liturgical Theology* (Minneapolis: Augsburg Fortress, 1993), 15. For further discussion see Gordon W. Lathrop, "A Rebirth of Images: On the Use of the Bible in Liturgy," *Worship* vol. 58, no. 4 (July 1984): 291-304.

8. *Lutheran Book of Worship* (Minneapolis and Philadelphia: Augsburg Publishing House and Board of Publications, Lutheran Church in America, 1978), 121-125.

9. All liturgical rites are connected, for all are part of the ongoing liturgy in the courts of heaven.

one becomes a part of the body of Christ, he or she becomes a part of God's saving history and is eternally connected to all that God has done, is doing, and promises to do. And then, just as in the Great Thanksgiving we have a full Trinitarian Prayer of Thanksgiving which, like Eucharistic Prayer I of *LBW*, begins *Holy God, mighty Lord, gracious Father*. What follows is a 20th century adaptation of Luther's "flood prayer" (*Sintflutgebet*).[10] The *LBW* takes Luther's prayer as a model and then includes language from the Roman Catholic blessing over the waters as well as the thanksgiving over the waters from the *Book of Common Prayer*.[11] One Lord, one faith, one baptism (Eph. 4:5-6): structurally we learn that there is only one church, and that a child is baptized a Christian, not a Presbyterian, nor a Lutheran, nor a Roman Catholic, but simply as one who now dwells in Christ's body crucified and risen from the dead.

Then the flood comes to us, a flood of images and figures, of incarnational reality and Holy Sacrament. *Holy God, mighty Lord, gracious Father, We give you thanks, for in the beginning*

---

10. "Almighty eternal God, who according to thy righteous judgment didst condemn the unbelieving world through the flood and in thy great mercy didst preserve believing Noah and his family, and who didst drown hardhearted Pharaoh with all his host in the Red Sea and didst lead thy people Israel through the same on dry ground, thereby prefiguring this bath of thy baptism, and who through the baptism of thy dear Child, our Lord Jesus Christ, hast consecrated and set apart the Jordan and all water as a salutary flood and rich and full washing away of sins: We pray through the same thy groundless mercy that thou wilt graciously behold this N. and bless him with true faith in the spirit so that by means of this saving flood all that has been born in him from Adam and which he himself has added thereto may be drowned in him and engulfed, and that he may be sundered from the number of the unbelieving, preserved dry and secure in the holy ark or Christendom, serve thy name at all times fervent in spirit and joyful in hope, so that with all believers he may be made worthy to attain eternal life according to thy promise; through Jesus Chris our Lord. Amen." Martin Luther, Order for Holy Baptism (1523) in *LW* 53:107-8.

11. Philip Pfatteicher, *Commentary on the Lutheran Book of Worship: Lutheran Liturgy in Its Ecumenical Context* (Minneapolis: Augsburg Fortress, 1990), 41.

your Spirit moved over the waters and you created heaven and earth.... the One who moved over the waters, the One who quenched the thirst of a discarded woman at a well, the One who created rivers teeming with life and meadows where sheep may safely graze, this God of all the ages is moving over the waters right now – for you.

All that is sinful in you, your rebellious nature itself will be drowned in a deluge, a flood. You need not fear that your sin is stronger than his love, your wickedness wider than his grace. No human being can withstand this tsunami: only those safely in the ark of his love. That ark is now the church and she will carry you through the stormiest of seas. He is saving you from these waters, not because you've done anything particularly right, but because it his way. He is who he is, and he is claiming you as his own. Your life is dependent upon his saving grace. The church, on God's behalf, is declaring to you that your life always has been and will always be in his hands, even when the forces of evil tell you otherwise. Just like he opened the sea for Moses and the children of Israel that they might worship him, so now he is giving you the path for your life, the life that he has wanted for you from the beginning of time, a life where your only desire is to live under him in his kingdom – where you desire what he desires for you: *love, joy, peace, patience, kindness, goodness, faithfulness, gentleness, and self-control* (Gal. 5:22-23). Receiving these biblical words in the context of thanksgiving at the very start of our life in faith is the pattern by which God intends for all of Scripture to come to us – which is then exactly what his Holy Spirit does – calling, gathering, enlightening, and sanctifying in the whole Christian church on earth. Holy baptism is the start of a holy life in a holy assembly, where the Holy Scriptures are received in faith.

And it was in a holy faith that Jesus, the Son of God, entered into the waters of the Jordan. Sinners were slithering along its muddy banks, but John's heart was leaping in his chest at the sight of this One (Mt. 3:14). Of all the biblical images proclaimed in this Prayer of Thanksgiving, the inclusion of Jesus' baptism in the Jordan is the clearest picture we have of the presence of the Holy Trinity in every page of God's Holy History. In the fullness of his humility and as a sign of our destiny, that through baptism we will be one with him until eternity, Jesus walks into the waters of repentance among sinners in need of cleansing, and the Spirit who hovered over the waters of creation comes again in the already ancient sign of the promised land ahead, in the form of a dove. No olive branch is needed now, for the Father's voice will reach forward to bring peace to a millennia of searching hearts, *This is my son, the beloved, with whom I am well pleased* (Mt. 3:17). From henceforth, Jesus, fully human, fully divine, will be bringing sinners to the Father's heart, and when we stray, the Spirit will come after us with a gale force to turn us back around (Acts 2:27-28; 11:15-18).

Then we come to the cross, the baptism of Jesus' own death and resurrection, which is the center of what we come to call the New Testament. Jesus uses the term (which is translated in English as), *the new testament in my blood*, long before there was a book we call the New Testament, and again we see Holy Scripture growing out of the liturgical assembly.[12] The cross and resurrection are the center of all Scripture, and all Scripture bears witness to this event. His last will and testament are given on Thursday night, a binding covenant which will define the identity and the future of all who receive it.[13] The sacrifice of his blood will be completed on

---

12. "There would have been and can now be no church without Israel's Scripture, but the church lived for over a century without having or needing a New Testament." Jenson, On the Inspiration of Scripture, 16.

13. "The word we render as 'testament' is, in Greek, *diatheke*. In the Septuagint, *diatheke* is used as the equivalent of the Hebrew word *berith*. Both *diatheke* and *berith* may be rendered more accurately in English as 'covenant' rather than as 'testament.' In ancient cultures, both words denote 'a widespread legal means by which the duties and privileges of kinship may be extended to another individual or group.' To the Jews of Jesus' time, a cov-

Friday (Heb 9:15; 12:24),[14] and the recipients of these benefits are yet coming through the baptismal waters. This is the way, the only way, to everlasting life, and so the "Flood Prayer" has even more to proclaim: Not only the woman at the well but the pools at Bethsaida (John 5:1-18) and Siloam (John 9:1-14), the cup of water given in Jesus' name (Mt. 10:42), the blood and water that flowed from his riven side (John 19:34), and the river in the heavenly city, flowing down crystalline and pure, like a high mountain stream cleansing inside and out (Rev. 22:1-2). Orthodox Theologian, Alexander Schmemann, goes so far to say that the reason God created water is so that we would be saved through it.[15] Water, without it there is no life on earth; water, the sign of eternal life.

Then, we are at last reminded of the command and promise of how disciples are made. In the 28th chapter of the Gospel according to St. Matthew, we hear: *Go, and make disciples of all nations, baptizing them in the name of the Father, and of the Son, and of the Holy Spirit and teaching them to obey all things whatsoever I commanded you* (Mt 28:19-20). This is the warrant

---

enant created a family bond where none had existed before.... A covenant was normally marked by a solemn ritual oath, sealed with a blood sacrifice, and often with a shared meal.... *Berith* was sometimes used to describe the ritual oath by which parties entered or renewed a covenant.... The ritual was so important to the parties of a covenant that it served as a shorthand term for their personal and collective identity. Thus, Saint Paul could refer to his fellow Jews as simply 'the circumcision'" (Colossians 4:11). Scott Hahn, *Consuming the Word: The New Testament and the Eucharist in the Early Church* (New York: Image, 2013), 17-18.

14. "What makes Good Friday's death a sacrifice, then, was the offering Jesus had made – in explicitly sacrificial terms, during his Last Supper with his disciples. There he made an offering of 'body' and 'blood.' He declared it to be his 'memorial,' a term (in Greek, *anamnesis*; in Hebrew, *zikkaron*) associated with the Temple's sacrificial liturgy. As he identified his action in terms of prophetic categories, most explicitly, the 'new covenant' of Jeremiah's oracle." Hahn, *Consuming the Word*, 25.

15. Alexander Schmemann, "Worship in a Secular Age," in *St. Vladimir's Theological Quarterly*, vol. 16, no. 1 (1972): 14.

that says water and the word: the washing that both mirrors everyday washing, the washing that is more than skin deep, the washing that tells of life being brought from the first waters, the washing that comes every time your sin is confessed and forgiven, the washing that will come when it's time for everything in this life to be swept away so that you may stand before the courts of heaven and enter in.

But there is still more to come in this Prayer of Thanksgiving, for just as Jesus spoke to Nicodemus, it is by water and the Spirit that we are born into eternal life (Jn. 3:5-6). And so we pray over this water which God has made for us, *Pour out your Holy Spirit,* just as we will pray over bread and wine at the Lord's Table, and just as we will pray with hands outstretched upon the head of one who is coming into the kingdom of God. And this prayer, as do all classic Trinitarian prayers, closes in the way Christians have prayed for centuries, adding our voices to all the faithful witnesses who have gone before us, *to* the Father, *through* the Son, *in* the Holy Spirit.

In the Order for Holy Baptism, the renunciation and the confession of faith follow, and then comes the washing, where the command of our Lord Jesus becomes the promise of our lives. The only way to walk in newness of life is to walk in the command and promise of the One who is the way, the truth, and the life, the One who is the resurrection and the life. *For if you have been united with him in a death like his you shall certainly be united with him in a resurrection like his* (Rom. 6:5). All that is "figured" for us in the law and the prophets, *Torah* and *Haftorah,* becomes the rule or canon of our lives on this day. All that is sung through the psalter – lament, praise, petition, and thanksgiving – becomes the canon of our lives on this day. All that is proclaimed in the Gospels, the Acts of the Apostles, the Epistles, and the Apocalypse of John becomes the canon of our lives on this day. All that is done to us and for us as we are drowned and brought forth becomes the holy shape of our lives on this day. *We were buried with him by baptism into death, so that as Christ was raised from the dead by the glory of the Father we too might walk in newness of life* (Rom. 6:4). St. Paul's words will be proclaimed at your death, but only because they are being proclaimed everyday of your baptized life: as you make the sign of the cross, as you profess your faith in God through the historic creeds, as you sing your children to sleep with songs of Jesus in their hearts, as you study his Holy Word in your homes and in your congregations, and as you get hands dirty in the mud-washed neighborhoods of the poor, and as you pray at the bedsides of beloved friends and family when all earthly hope is gone. Receiving this life, this beautiful life, in thanksgiving, shapes everything you are and everything you do, for it is to be done to the glory of God, your Father, which is the true meaning of the doxological life as you present your bodies as a living sacrifice, holy and acceptable to God (Rom 1:2).

And now having come through the waters, hands are placed on the head of the one who is being washed, and a prayer of thanksgiving and intercession is offered, a practice that goes back to the *Apostolic Tradition*.[16] Thanksgiving for an eternal freedom, for Christ has set us free (Galatians 5:1) and intercession for the Holy Spirit to descend (Acts 2). Think again of figure, reality, and sacrament, and hear now the prophecy of Isaiah, *There shall come forth a shoot from the stump of Jesse, and a branch shall grow out of his roots. And the Spirit of the Lord shall rest upon him, the spirit of wisdom and understanding, the spirit of counsel and might, the spirit of knowledge and the fear of the Lord. And his delight shall be in the fear of the Lord* (Is. 11:13). And think of our Lord Jesus upon whom the Spirit descends, and who, when called upon in the synagogue to read another

---

16. "The prayer for the Spirit (no. 246) is a revision of the prayer from the sixth-century Gelasian Sacramentary, which derives from the third-century *Apostolic Tradition* of Hippolytus. The enumeration of the seven gifts of the Spirit had perhaps been made in Rome in the fourth century. Pfatteicher, *Commentary on the Lutheran Book of Worship*, 53.

passage about the Spirit in the scroll Isaiah begins with, The Spirit of the Lord is upon me, (Is 6:1:1) and who then proclaims that this word is fulfilled in our hearing. And now as each newborn soldier of the crucified is claimed by Christ, and in a moment will wear his seal upon their brow (*LBW* 177), a seal that marks ownership – eternal ownership[17] – we are so bold to ask that the Holy Spirit will fill the life of each member in Christ's living body, that Isaiah's prophecy would be the content of every thought, word, and deed of our lives, and our lives will be a delight to the Lord our God.

II. Eucharist

The Lord's Supper, Holy Communion, Eucharist, The Table of the Lord, The Mass, The Supper of the Lamb, The Sacrament of the Altar: We know this Holy Meal by many names. We remember that *in the night in which he was betrayed, our Lord Jesus took bread and gave thanks, broke it and gave it to his disciples to eat* (1 Cor. 11:23-24). We remember and then we receive his crucified and risen body into our bodies, which already belong to him. *Your ancestors ate manna in the desert, but this is the bread of life from heaven. Eat this bread. Drink this cup. Come to me and never be hungry. Eat this bread. Drink this cup. Come to me and you will not thirst* (*WOV* 709). When Jesus lifts the cup of the everlasting covenant, he calls it the *New Testament* in his blood, and when the 27 books that bear witness to his suffering and death, his very dying and rising are later given the name *New*

---

17. "The word *sphragis* in ancient times designated the object with which a mark was stamped, or else the mark made by this object. So *sphragis* was the word for the seal used to impress a mark on wax.... These seals were used especially to seal official documents and wills. So St. Paul uses the symbol when he tells the Corinthians that they 'are the seal of the apostolate of the Lord' (1 Cor. 9:2), that is to say that they are the authentic sign of it. But more particularly—and here we come to baptismal symbolism—the word sphragis was used for the mark with which an owner marked his possessions." Daniélou, *The Bible and the Liturgy*, 55.

Testament, they have at their center this ritual act. These 27 were understood to be liturgical books that bore witness to his sacrifice, the New Covenant in his eternal love. Holy books were to be read aloud as the assembly received the New Testament in his blood, holy books that witness to his death on a cross and his glorious rising from the dead.[18] As they were continually spoken in the assembly, first as eyewitness accounts, then as memoirs, then in the form we know as the Gospels, the process of canonization of both Scripture and the liturgy completed each other.[19]

As the first generations of disciples trusted in the promise of his presence, they, like Cleopas and his companion on the road to Emmaus, recognized their Lord in the breaking of the bread (Luke 24:30-31). The telling of his life, his ministry, his incarnation, his death, and his resurrection were part of that ritual act. The reading of memoirs of the apostles, the letters of Peter and Paul (and of the law and the prophets) was the context in which his sacramental presence was

---

18. "What is proclaimed in the assembly are texts taken from the canonical corpus of the scriptures. But these texts, which must be respected according to their very letter (i.e., in the inescapable actuality of their historical and cultural otherness), are in some way taken out of their state of death by the voice of the reader, who thus expresses symbolically (sacramentally) the essence of the word alive for the 'today' of each generation (cf. Deuteronomy)." Louis-Marie Chauvet. "What Makes the Liturgy Biblical?—Texts," *Studia Liturgica* 22 (1992): 127.

19. "When the last books (of the New Testament) were written, they described a church already well established, with a developed ritual life. Indeed, it was in the middle of the church's liturgy that the first [gentile] Christian congregations encountered the Scriptures of the Old Testament. It was for proclamation in the liturgy that the books of the New Testament were written.... Even then those books were not known as the New Testament.... The documents gradually took on that name ... because of their liturgical proximity to the covenant sacrifice, the Eucharist. They were the *only* books approved to be read in the Eucharistic liturgy, and they were canonized for that very reason. Thus, precisely as *liturgical books* they were called the New Testament." Hahn, *Consuming the Word*, 40-41.

given Sunday after Sunday, the day of his rising.[20] The proximity between that which Jesus called the *New Testament in my blood*, and that which the assembly believed to be the spoken Word of God (from the Spirit hovering over the waters of creation to the Spirit being poured out on all flesh), that proximity became the mark of authenticity for these Holy Witnesses to the love of God for all those whom he had made. What was to become the Canon of the Bible came from Jesus' own declaration that the sacrifice of his life was, in effect, a covenantal sacrifice, as had been Moses' sacrifices on behalf of God's people (Ex. 24:4-8). But in this sacrifice, once for all (Hebrews 10: 12-14), God intended for the whole world to be made anew in his never-ending love. As Jesus called his disciples to *Do this in remembrance of me*, and they did, such remembrance took shape in both hearing the word and in sacramental action—word and earthly element according to the command of the LORD.

The writings that became canonized as Holy Scripture flowed from this action of remembering and eating in his name, for in this ritual gathering the living word of God was remembered and proclaimed doxologically as the faithful glorified God through their adoration of him and their dependence upon his promises.

---

20. "We read a text from the gospel, not in order to recapture the time when independent tradition units circulated in the Christian communities, but in order to set the pericope we read next to the passion and resurrection of Christ held forth now in the Supper. Hence reading the individual pericopes and then celebrating the Supper present us with a skein of images reinterpreting images which is the very pattern of the Gospel books themselves. The Sunday texts are not then understood aright unless they are understood as leading to that Supper. The hierarchy of readings in the Sunday eucharist may then be thought of as a primary example of a skein of images reborn. And the lessons for feast days may frequently be seen as a kind of palimpsest of images, image written upon image." Lathrop, *A Re-birth of Images, Worship*, 296.

We still do this in the very structure of the liturgy, from the Entrance Rite to the Dismissal, the proclamation of the law, prophets, psalms, and apostles that surrounds the ritual meal. From invocation to benediction, the Divine Liturgy is a structural whole, each smaller word and gesture play a role in a larger event, just like floorboards and skylight are part of what makes a building whole. We've inherited a pattern, a scaffolding with some scriptural elements that became standardized in the first millennium of the church and some scriptural elements that were variable by festival and season. Not only did the church inherit a cycle of annual festivals from Judaism, she inherited a ritual understanding that such a cycle was essential for the faithfulness of the children of God, whose lives were part of the whole creation, sun and moon, and shining stars, winged birds and fish of the sea. Human beings are part of God's creation, the God who orders the seasons, who makes the sun to rise out of the dawn, and the stillness of the night hours in which to rock our babies to rest. God gives us seedtime and harvest, the rain and the land itself, his good earth, and in the regularity of his holy rhythms, faithful Israel learns to give thanks for his protection and his unceasing grace.

Within that movement of chronological time (*chronos*) God has made specific and particularly scandalizing moves to save his people (*kairos*). Moses, Abraham, Zipporah, Shiphrah, Hannah, David, Sarah, Rachel, Isaac, and a host of others believed that this One God who set all life in motion was leading them into the future he was preparing for them. So into the festivals that thanked God for daily sustenance, festivals which were based on the regular cycles of the moon in the night sky, there came festivals of thanksgiving for specific acts in salvation history. These seven festivals of sustenance and salvation: *Pesach, Chag Hamotzi, Yom Habbikurim, Shavu'ot, Yom Teru'ah, Yom Kippur, Sukkot* (Passover, Unleavened Bread, First Fruits, Pentecost, Trumpets, Atonement, Tabernacles) are the model from which the Christian liturgical calendar began. The liturgical calendar of faithful Israel is a doxological catechism that teaches us the content of the faith as it binds our lives together in a continual ritual renewal of God's new covenant with us.[21]

With that annual cycle of festivals came appointed readings in addition to an annual cycle of daily readings. Law and prophets, *Torah* and *Haftorah*, the words on the scroll were the holy residue of the speaking of God, until Jesus, as was his custom, unrolled the scroll of the prophet Isaiah and said, *This word is fulfilled in your hearing* (Luke 4:2). All that had been pre-figured was now a reality, and while lectionary assignments have changed through the centuries (they have not been set in stone) they have still been ordered around the annual cycle of festivals with which they are associated. God acted, and his actions were written down in order to be spoken again, year after year. Accompanying the annual ritual cycle of Christian festivals there have been one, two, and three year cycles of reading, each one connected to the ways in which God has made himself known in saving his people.[22]

---

21. "The fixing of the liturgy in both [Judaism and Christianity], is indebted to the same anxieties about setting boundaries as the fixing of the scriptures. This is reflected in the directions for the Passover festival in Exodus 12f., where elements of the story and the ritual are so woven into one another that neither can exist any longer without the other. Structurally, the same thing applies to the Passion and Easter narratives, insofar as the Synoptic writers hand on the central text of the gradually developing Eucharistic celebration (the 'institution narrative') in the framework of the passion story to provide in narrative form a rationale for this form of worship.... The intertwined development of Christian Scripture and liturgy could be described in this way: the Passover ensures the telling of the Passion and Easter narrative and at the same time this sacrificial narrative, with the new Passover ritual, gives shape to the developing Christian liturgy with the ritual sacrificial action." Klaus-Peter Jorns, "Liturgy: Cradle of Scripture?" *Studia Liturgica* 22 (1992), 28. Anecdotally, Hahn tells of "One of the great modern rabbis, Samson Raphel Hirsch, [who] once said that the catechism of the Jew is the calendar. Though we Christians do have useful catechisms, the statement is doubly true for us as well." Hahn, *Consuming the Word*, 83.

22. The RCL has a doxological hermeneutic.

As the appointed passages are read aloud in the midst of the scaffolding of the scriptural passages that comprise the spoken/sung text of the Eucharistic liturgy, an auditory building, from concrete foundation to open third-story window, is created.

The preaching of the Word follows the oral proclamation of the Holy Scriptures, and through such preaching, the mighty acts of God to which the Holy Scriptures are witnesses, are given to us in faith.[23] Preaching in the Sunday assembly is a performative doxological eucharistic exegesis of the biblical text. Just as in the hearing of the text, the ink on the page is made incarnate in our lives, so through faithful preaching, the witness of the text gives glory to God as the preacher recounts what God has done, what God is doing, and of course, what he promises to do. Biblical preaching as a liturgical act does not simply lead an assembly to learn information, as one would learn facts from a textbook. Biblical preaching leads an assembly to worship God, Father, Son, and Holy Spirit, who has called these people his own and who has made himself known through his word.

Please note that we don't preach from the Bhagavad Gita or the Quran, or the Rubaiyat of Oman Khayyam. We do not and could not proclaim that they are "The Word of the Lord." They have many things to say of interest but they are not witnesses to the resurrection of Jesus Christ which, of course, the Bible is. Neither do we sing hymns in our liturgical assemblies that glorify creation, or self, or race, or nation. The hymns that we sing within our liturgical structure, par-

---

23. "Thus, for the most obvious instance of the Spirit's ways with Scripture, he inspires Scripture in that he provides it to preachers – of various sorts – in the form of texts, whether by the regulated proceedings of the church or otherwise. We may begin with a maxim more or less like what is usually said: the text is there to enable an identity of the sermon's message with that of the prophets and apostles." Jenson, *On the Inspiration of Scripture*, 60-61.

ticularly the *de tempore* hymn (the hymn of the day), work in concert with the word of the preacher so that as the assembly becomes of one voice in its lament or praise, or as it calls for or expresses a repentant heart, or as it sings in ways that words alone cannot express, filled with the sighs of the Holy Spirit. Through the liturgical structure, the proclamation of the Word, the singing of the faith that is in you, the hand outstretched to receive Christ's body into your own, you are coming to know the Bible doxologically: You are coming to know the Scriptures in their natural context, the church alive in prayer, praise, and thanksgiving.

And so now one final look at a few more of the Holy Words that are both proclaimed in Scripture and the Eucharistic liturgy: the *Sursum Corda*, the Proper Preface, the *Sanctus*, and the Eucharistic Prayer.

> *The Lord be with you. And also with you.*
> *Lift up your hearts. We lift them to the Lord.*
> *Let us give thanks to the Lord our God. It is right to give*
> *him thanks and praise.*

With the same biblical salutation that precedes the Collect, the presider calls out to the congregation, *The Lord be with you.* Take a moment to think of all the places in Scripture where God's presence is with his people. Think of all the times in your life when that was the one word you needed to hear. Just as the Angel Gabriel spoke to a young woman named Mary, *The Lord is with you*, so he is coming to you. Next we're called upon to open our bodies to receive him. *Lift up your hearts.* Take that breath in and your rib cage expands, your heart is thus exposed to God. In your vulnerability, there is nothing you can hide. Then fully trusting that your life is in his hands, you are called upon to give thanks. No matter what's happened in that day or that week, what trials or temptations you have faced, what sorrows you have wept, the call is still to give thanks to the One who has promised to be with you in it all.

The Proper Preface then joins your thanks and praise to the praise that is continually sounded in the heavens. It is addressed to the Father, through the Son, and it is tied to the festival or season, often through a biblical phrase or allusion, which help us to understand the heart of the festival and of the appointed Scriptures proclaimed on that day. One clear example of this is the Proper Preface for the Ascension. Forty days after his resurrection, Jesus is taken up into the heavens, and the Preface, in the words of 2 Peter 1:4, tells us why, *so that he might make us partakers of his divine nature*. On Ascension Day we celebrate the completion of his work of salvation for the sake of whole world. As we hear and believe the promise of his Ascension, we understand that our own lives are now lived in kingdom time, eternal time, the time where God's glory has no end. All that we do and all that we are is to give God glory, for this is what we are made for – to be partakers of his divine nature. The doxological proclamation of the biblical text is the key to experiencing the unity of Scripture and liturgy.

The Eucharistic Prayer comes to us through the centuries in a multiplicity of forms and more than one historic controversy (which is a wider discussion than this presentation). Yet as we focus today on how we come to know the Bible through the liturgy, I want you simply to think about Trinitarian structure, biblical texts, and the actions of Jesus at the Last Supper. Using *LBW* Eucharistic Prayer I as a model that you may be familiar with, take a moment to become a theological detective. It opens with a three-fold acclamation that tells us of the holiness, the strength, and the grace of the One whom we call Father. It tells that he set the universe in motion and that he will be there at the consummation of all things. We hear how he created the universe and how he called Abraham to faith. It tells of salvation history, of God's Holy History through the prophets, until the arrival of his Son who proclaimed his kingdom and was obedient to his will, even to giving his life. If you take the time, you will find a biblical reference for every line of this prayer, and it is clear that through such praying, the Canon of Scripture is being given to you doxologically, so that you may believe that Jesus is, indeed, the Savior of the world, and that through his sacrifice – once for all – he is binding himself to you in a covenant of eternal love. As in the *Sanctus*, which also uses both Old Testament and New Testament passages (Isaiah 6:2, Mt. 21:9 and Ps. 188:26), Holy Scripture is again being simultaneously prayed and proclaimed. The words of institution tell *what* he did on that night, and the Prayer of Thanksgiving *does* what he did as he gave thanks to his Father.

> *Baruch atah Adonai eloheinu melech ha-alom hamotzi lechem min ha-aretz.*
> Blessed are you O LORD our God, king of the universe, who brings forth bread from the earth.
> *Baruch atah Adonai eloheinu melech ha-aolm bor-ay peri ha-gafen.*
> Blessed are you, O LORD our God, king of the universe, creator of the fruit of the vine.

In placing the Words of Institution in the midst of the proclamation of God's Holy History from the beginning of time, the assembly learns that the only way to understand the Old Testament is through the New, and that the New Testament is of a woven cloth with the Old, with Jesus Christ as the center of it all.

Then hearing that this New Testament, this New Covenant was given for us, we (and that is, for all of humanity) who once cried out for his death, now cry out the glorious acclamation of his resurrected life; *Christ has died. Christ is risen, Christ will come again.* Our remembrance gives honor to the apostolic witness as we look for the day when all who have been invited to the banquet will be gathered into one (Rev. 19:6-9).

Finally, in the beauty and balance of a Trinitarian proclamation we call for the Holy Spirit to form our lives in the shape of praise that will carry us into the future that God is preparing for those who love him. Our great high priest after the Order of Melchizedek is yet praying for us, for which we give thanks in an explosion of praise, *Through him, with him, in him, in the unity of the Holy Spirit, all honor and glory is yours, almighty Father, now and forever. Amen.*

And then our resurrected Lord teaches us to pray as he has taught his disciples on a hillside, *Our Father who art in heaven, Hallowed be thy name.* As Holy Baptism was the start of a holy life in a holy assembly where the Holy Scriptures are received in faith, the call to join in this prayer of our Lord Jesus which names the God of Abraham, the God of Isaac, and the God of Jacob as our Father, this prayer in which the tablets of the law that Moses brought down the mountain are given to the church doxologically, i.e., in the form of a prayer, so this prayer opens our hearts to a fullness of thanksgiving for every breath, for every grain of wheat, for every cool drop of water, for every glance that comes our way in love, for every kiss on a tiny scraped knee, and for every caress that cradles the cheek of a dying friend. Through such prayer, the crumb and the sip that follow carry the power and might that created the universe, for in the body and blood of our resurrected Lord comes the promise that God is creating the world anew. With such a love, we can at last give thanks for this day in which he is making his eternal goodness known to us. Amen.

The Ethics of Sex, Marriage, and the Family

Christopher R. Seitz

Personal Remarks

When Carl Braaten e-mailed me to participate in this conference, likely he knew Charleston would conjure up memories of past events and make the invitation all the more enticing. The Anglican Communion Institute hosted regular January conferences in Charleston for about ten years, beginning in 1996. We started a three-book series on the Nicene Creed, The Ten Commandments and the Lord's Prayer, with contributions by Carl, Robert Jenson, and David Yeago—from the Lutheran Tribe—as well as Methodist, Roman Catholic, Reformed, Orthodox and Free Church authors.[1] "The Future for a New Ecumenism" was one book's optimistic subtitle. But church politics overtook us, and looking back it seems like a slow-moving train wreck was only beginning, leaving us with the break-up and carnage all of us in our various Christian tribes are now surveying. I started my teaching career 30 years ago as the first non-Lutheran to teach at the seminary in Philadelphia, and ate a frequent lunch at 2900 Queen Lane at the then Fortress Press. So your world and my own denominated world have inter-

---

1. C. Seitz, ed., *Nicene Christianity: The Future for a New Ecumenism* (Grand Rapids: Brazos, 2001); Carl E. Braaten and C. Seitz, eds., *"I am the Lord Your God": Christian Reflections on the Ten Commandments* (Grand Rapids: Eerdmans, 2005).

sected for many years. Though most of my PhD students at Toronto now come from the Missouri Synod Lutheran branch, I have never felt far from the wider Lutheran universe, here and in Germany, which under the hand of God is now not what you or I might have expected 30 years ago.

General Challenges

I want to mention a couple of challenges before I begin. They inform what I will say and guide the selection of what I choose to focus on. I recall speaking on homosexuality at Brite Divinity School in the late 90s and vowing never to do another conference on the topic, whose format featured a "diversity of viewpoints." Something had obviously broken in our appeal to Scripture that would not be resolved by everyone trying a bit harder or with more charity.[2]

Secondly, the topic as sketched out seems to require the services of a paid-up ethicist and I am a biblical scholar. So I am not going to wander too far from my own area of training. But I will try to embrace the challenge in this specific way. I will take ethics to mean the way the biblical teaching from Genesis to Revelation takes practical form in our world of living the gospel faith. Unavoidably, I believe that takes us straight to the marriage rites of the church. I know these differ amongst our Christian tribes, but they have had far more in common in their various present guises than ones that will soon be upon us. We may disagree about whether Christian marriage is a sacrament and what that means, but we can all agree that standing before God, making solemn vows and receiving the church's blessing, constitutes an ethical act. Something is being agreed to, before God. And most importantly, what warrants the blessing of God Almighty is being set forth, heard by all, witnessed to and affirmed on those terms and not others.

---

2. The conference papers were published as David Balch, ed., *Homosexuality, Science, and the "Plain Sense" of Scripture* (Grand Rapids: Eerdmans, 2000).

The marriage rite in the Episcopal *Book of Common Prayer* (*BCP*) will guide my ethical reflections because that is the tradition I am familiar with. I would be surprised if the basic warrants and contours, biblically rooted and biblically norming, were not familiar to you on similar terms.[3] An important point is thereby registered. Mine will not be an examination of the crucial character of this or that marriage rite, as somehow more decisive than the scriptural landscape that gives rise to them. Every marriage rite assumes as much as it expresses explicitly, through its specific language and form. The relationship, then, between the whole scriptural landscape and what it expresses on this subject and what the rites functioning in the church foreground is a symbiotic one. A good rite follows what has been traditionally called the rule of faith, and the rule of faith is a faithful, proportional, comprehensive coming-to-boil of what Scripture as a whole commends, under the lordship of Jesus Christ, who is its everlasting Word. Christian Ethics points to that place where Scripture, in accordance with the rule of faith, comes into life and practice. This means when Christians make marriage vows in a rite of the church, an ethical form of life is being embraced by us, bigger than us, and worthy of being bigger because warranted by God in creation, in Christ, and in his church from all eternity.

I am prepared to speak on this topic yet again because we now face a particular challenge in our culture and in the church in understanding Christian marriage and family. The word "marriage" is likely to be/is being taken over by culture and altered in respect of the goods formerly implied thereby. This won't be the first time language of the church has been bent to new purpose, and it won't be the last. But that gives the church the responsibility to be clear about what it means

---

3. See my comments on "tacit knowledge" and the *Book of Common Prayer* in *The Character of Christian Scripture* (Grand Rapids: Baker Academic, 2011), 173-90.

by the word "marriage" when it finds its place within the ethical decision making inherent in a solemn rite, with Scripture readings, solemn charges, vows, prayers, and blessing. It is to this 'marriage' that I will be speaking, and not to newer efforts to commandeer the word and alter the "estate" to which we have been called by Scripture through the rites of the church's ruled life.

Two final comments. Anticipating my conclusion, I believe it is clear that churches will alter marriage rites consistent with their altered understanding. They will create what they call gender-neutral rites, or they will seek to make a progressive new rite range alongside a former one, or they will eliminate a former one altogether and aggressively so; all three options are on the table.

In the light of this it is important to keep in mind and heart that what they cannot succeed in doing is erasing from the church's life and time the logic and ethical contours of a former one I will be working with today. They will believe they will be doing that, but in point of fact, ethically speaking, they cannot. Rather, what they will succeed in doing is not so much changing a rite, but changing the nature of the church into a very different one, one which will no longer be ruled and normed on these ritual terms and not by others. In spite of all that, the rites we have traditionally used and the scriptural and dominical warrants they presuppose will not vanish from the earth. Those who wish to enter into this traditional marriage estate, and understand it as the arena in which God's blessing is made possible in Christ, by action of the Holy Spirit, will continue to do so and will thereby bear witness to a specific set of scriptural convictions. One may change a word. One may create a new self-understanding and call it church. One cannot vaporize an understanding of marriage whose sacred character will outlive semantic changes.

Second. In so much of the rhetoric of the modern and post-modern world we find the appeal to something called identity. Not a verbal but a nominal state of affairs, called "being gay," or "LGBTi." Is this state of affairs socially constructed and so generated by specific cultural conditions, and if so, is it a desirable outcome or one that is corrigible of change, given other possible constructive forces? I believe this topic represents the coal-face of our modern and postmodern evaluation, and it is a deeply ethical question we are likely too in-the-middle-of- things for time in God's hand to have rendered a sufficiently clear verdict. But there is also a deeply biblical question about what the term "identity" might mean for those of us Paul describes as having died and been buried in Christ, whose present identity, as men and as women, is hid with him.

Do we speak far too confidently than God would allow us, in Christ, of any identity, as finally determinative of who we are in him? Perhaps the most Christian answer to the question of identity is permanently to confess that we do not fully know who we are, because day by day, as men and women, we are being made new creations in him, if indeed we are allowing his life to be the measure of who we are becoming. An entire lecture could be dedicated to this very important ethical question.[4] I have said enough to indicate my own deep skepticism about whether there is something like a clear "gay" or "straight" identity, much less one that could be determinative in any major way for what it means to be a Christian.

The Character of the Biblical Witness and Christian Marriage

Now to the heart of the present challenge, which I believe is a familiar one in the ancient church as well.

---

4. See the perceptive evaluation of Oliver O'Donovan in *Self, World, and Time: Ethics as Theology* (Vol. 1; Grand Rapids: Eerdmans, 2013) and *The Church in Crisis: Homosexuality and the Anglican Communion* (Eugene, Oregon: Cascade Books, 2008).

Every opponent of Christianity – real or perceived – was an ardent Scripture reader. We know this clearly from reading the works of the early church fathers. There we see steady and sustained engagement with rival views of Scripture and interpretation, as they struggle to defend the church's faith and practice on the basis of the Scriptures. It was said one time, "there is no such thing as an impious heretic." It could equally be said, "there was no false or misleading account of Christian faith that did not take the form of an argument from Scripture" – and how Scripture delivers its proper sense.

Three examples:

1. The Gnostics liked Scripture because it expressed experiences of ascent and higher knowledge they judged to be rather weak examples of their own. Indeed for the Gnostics, after the Bible things got better in their own land of religious experience. The Bible shows us something experiential and points to it out beyond its own limited range. Beyond that, it is dispensable. It is a metaphor pool. A set of spiritual suggestions. Not a source but a resource.[5]

---

5. Paul's reference to an ascent to heavenly perspective was evocative for them. "When, however, they are confuted from the Scriptures, they turn round and accuse these same Scriptures, as if they were not correct, nor of authority, and [assert] that they are ambiguous, and that the truth cannot be extracted from them by those who are ignorant of tradition. For [they allege] that the truth was not delivered by means of written documents, but *vivâ voce*: wherefore also Paul declared, "But we speak wisdom among those that are perfect, but not the wisdom of this world." And this wisdom each one of them alleges to be the fiction of his own inventing, forsooth; so that, according to their idea, the truth properly resides at one time in Valentinus, at another in Marcion, at another in Cerinthus, then afterwards in Basilides, or has even been indifferently in any other opponent, who could speak nothing pertaining to salvation. For every one of these men, being altogether of a perverse disposition, depraving the system of truth, is not ashamed to preach himself" (Ireneaus, *Against Heresies*, Book III, Chapter 2).

2. Marcion and his followers liked the Bible because it had some books that were decidedly and obviously better than others. Once one cleared out the undergrowth, the pure gospel could be found in Galatians and Luke (shorn of infancy narratives and references to Moses and the Prophets in Luke 24). On this account, not all of Scripture was usable or *intended to be usable*. Once one identified what kind of Jesus Jesus was, and what kind of God he bespoke, the rest could be dispensed with. This economical stripped-down Jesus was in many ways easier to package and sell. Marcion we know had quite a following. In sum, for them the Bible is correct but just in selected parts and only after extensive pruning.[6]

3. Arius liked Scripture because read properly it confirmed the most accurate way to describe a high Christ and an even higher godhead, thus preserving the oneness and transcendence of the God to which Scripture otherwise referred. "He created me the first of his ways with the world" was a critical assertion from Proverbs 8:22 and believe it or not, it formed the main arena of exegetical debate over creedal language, as it would take form at Nicaea, "God from God, light from light ... of one substance with the Father." No, Arius said, that is not what Scripture said, either at Proverbs 8 or elsewhere. Arius was a literalist who did not

---

6. "But, again, when we refer them to that tradition which originates from the apostles, [and] which is preserved by means of the succession of presbyters in the churches, they object to tradition, saying that they themselves are wiser not merely than the presbyters, but even than the apostles, because they have discovered the unadulterated truth. For [they maintain] that the apostles intermingled the things of the law with the words of the Saviour; and that not the apostles alone, but even the Lord Himself, spoke as at one time from the Demiurge, at another from the intermediate place, and yet again from the Pleroma, but that they themselves, indubitably, unsulliedly, and purely, have knowledge of the hidden mystery: this is, indeed, to blaspheme their Creator after a most impudent manner! It comes to this, therefore, that these men do now consent neither to Scripture nor to tradition" (Irenaeus, III.2).

like Scripture to be read as a complex totality, its sum greater than its parts. It is instead a book of discrete parts to be read as literally and discretely as possible.[7] The roots of this view likely go back to the School of Antioch.[8]

If we are going to reflect on a theme like "The Ethics of Sex, Marriage and Family," and presume to be doing so on the basis of the canon of Scripture, we must be prepared to accept a cardinal reality. To speak of Christian Ethics is to speak of Scripture in action, in the lived life of Christian formation and catechesis. Increasingly, very few progressives dismiss the scriptural record on sex, marriage and family. Some of course still do. They are bold to proclaim that the biblical witness is not just wrong in its parts (Genesis 1-3 as ancient Hebrew musing, Paul as wrong or speaking about something else, Jesus as all loving and disinterested in a modern phenomenon like gayness, which exists in a time frame the Bible does not nor could ever be expected to comprehend). The Bible is wrong, outdated, or just not addressing the matter of the challenge of new understandings of sex and human thriving, altogether. If it gets things right, it does so accidentally or inferentially, like the proverbial blind hog finding an acorn.

I mention this right up front because, as with the early church, what we now see is something else: a heavy assault *mounted from within Christian circles themselves* on prior understandings of the estate of marriage and its goods. Not from cultural despisers or secularists, but from those who purport to argue that their new understanding is indeed scriptural after all. Many secular and religious proponents of same-sexuality had concluded earlier that marriage was a patriarchal invention that no card-carrying proponent of sexual libera-

---

7. What David Yeago has here referred to the "pea-shucking" model of interpretation.

8. See the very illuminating essay of C.F. Burney, "Christ as the ΑΡΧΗ of Creation (Prov. viii 22, Col. i 15–18, Rev. iii 14)," *JTS* 27 (1926): 160–77.

tion – gay or straight – ought to go near. Inside Christian circles, this has changed.

So alongside those dubious about Scripture having anything to say, accidentally or properly, are those who argue that their new understanding of sexuality is somehow biblical after all. In this sense, the debate over marriage, sex and family is one in which both sides, or several sides, all appeal to Scripture. That is not unlike the early church examples just cited. So we must ask: What account of Scripture is it that has been brought to bear on our present and older understandings of sex, marriage, and family. Because of its scale, depth, and complex two-Testament character, Scripture is infinitely capable of producing multiple interpretations. Irenaeus used the image of a mosaic. One receives a gift of Scripture with all its myriad pieces, and the goal of interpretation is to see the face of the king, Jesus Christ, when all the pieces are properly and proportionally assembled. But equally, one could toss out pieces that do not seem to fit what one is looking for. Or one could assemble them and produce a fox, or a mirror of one's own self: our needs and rights and our individual paths to thriving. Gregory spoke of Scripture as a river in which infants could wade and elephants swim, at one and the same time. But he could equally have said, elephants drown and infants plumb false depths.

The church fathers appealed to a rule of faith when it came to proper interpretation of Scripture. Much of the rule wanted to clarify that the Scriptures of Israel, over their total warp and woof, spoke of Christ.[9] He was the word to patriarch, lawgiver, prophet, the word that brought a good creation into being, one with the father. "In the beginning (*arche*) was the word" rhyming with "in beginning – in *arche*, in Christ – God created the heavens and earth." John 1 and Colossians 1

---

9. See "The Rule of Faith, Hermeneutics, and the Character of Christian Scripture," in *Character*, 191-203.

were telling us what the referents of the Old Testament truly were in the light of the Incarnation's filling full of them. In *arche*, in beginning the Word, rhyming with *bereshith*, in beginning, in Christ, God created the heavens and the earth. The triune God at work in his own special way inside Israel's Scriptures, under cover within the privileged life God shared with the people of Israel. The *logos asarkos* – the word not yet made flesh – alive within the first testamental witness, because one with the only Lord God. In the language of Martin Luther, "Christ Jesus it is He, LORD Sabaoth his name, from age to age the same."

But several other things the rule would be seen to do. It ruled out pitting Scripture against itself, so as to produce hotter or colder parts, some then to be rejected as false parts. It required that the totality of the witness be held in creative tension in one lordly and coherent whole. It asked that prayer and humility accompany reading, because the difficult parts were likely to be where we would most learn, reliant now on a higher teacher than our first likes or instincts.

Sometimes their appeal to the rule of faith sounds like the rule that the faithful possess and live by, and which we simply do not recognize in your reading of Scripture or your account of Christ or his church. That is, it sounds like something is missing or wrong or dangerous in what you are proposing, and we know that because it collides with our own present practices and handling of Scripture. A kind of "what we have you do not have" and therefore it lacks the right rule. Catholic faith is not monolithic, but it exists within a circle outside of which you have strayed. Through attenuation, selection, wrong priority, higher spiritual ascent beyond the apostolic witness, rejection of major parts, a refusal to countenance the need to be taught, favorite books, and making the first testament Christ-less. Someone else's religion en route, maybe, but only partially, if at all, to a new religion.

How the faithful sensed these outside-the-rule-of-faith threats also arose as on collision with early baptismal rites, the preaching of the church, its sacramental self-understanding in the form of emergent rites and practices, its liturgical life in time, all emanating from the Scripture's total impress on the church as the *Logos* alive via the Holy Spirit.

This brings me to my first main biblical/ritual point. The Bible exists in relationship to the church's ruled life, which gives expression to its totality, its order, the fittingness of its parts. We have marriage rites. We ought to be able to see in them the rule of faith ordering how Scripture comes to boil. When we look at them, what account of Scripture do they provide?

I want to mention four components that are either given clear expression or are assumed.

The first arises in the conjunction of Genesis 1 and Christ's teaching in Matthew 19: male and femaleness as integral to the purposes of God in creation. God creates by bringing into being by his Word, Jesus Christ, and by ordering. day and night. Waters above waters below. Big light and lesser light. Male and female.

Within the modern debate, various conservative readers have sought to see in the Genesis account some deep structure of binary or complementary creational order. This could be a possible deduction, but it runs the risk of abstraction. The verbs used in Genesis 1 are not all the same from day to day. There is "create." There is "let there be." There is "separate" (five times). There is "gather." Some binary separations emerge as a bulwark against the chaotic "formless and void" over which the Spirit of God brooded.

On the fifth day living creatures of various kinds are brought forth and for the first time the word "blessing" appears, strikingly, in conjunction with the command to be fruitful and multiply. Now we are not speaking of ordered separation that will remain permanent and fixed – creation versus chaos – but of separations in the forms of species that nevertheless come together and propagate, in the light of God's blessing them.

Day six forms the denouement not simply because God announces through a first-time "very good" it to be so, but also because the creatures blessed and so capable of multiplying, we learn, are to be overseen in a special way by the male and female separated pair that are blessed and commanded to be fruitful and multiply. This humankind, this very good creation, is male and female, in the image of God. The fundamental act of differentiation is somehow mysteriously grounded in God's own character. God creates everything through every day through his Word, *arche*, with the Spirit of God mysteriously and sacramentally present. Christ is the true image and likeness of God. Male and female are created with reference to him, and in some sense mirroring the differentiation of the One God who is a fellowship of Father, Son and Holy Spirit, in overcoming love.

The Rule of Faith understands the New Testament's (NT) penetration into the literal sense deliverances of Genesis 1 to be faithful purchases on the eternal truth there imprinted. And they do this in no small part because in the NT, in Matthew 19:3-8, Christ refers to the "from the beginning" purposes of God as eternally expressed in Genesis 1 and inseparably connected to Genesis 2. Ephesians 5:31 and 1 Corinthians 6 track along this same exegetical logic. The Rule of Faith sees to it, then, that the parts of Scripture rhyme with each other. The Genesis 1 account tells of creation through the Word, through *arche*, and it is not a Hebrew myth, a past word trapped inside a history of religion (the "P" source), but a Word speaking to Israel and over Israel to the church and the created world itself eternally. Even subsequent adjustments concerning divorce, such as are referred to in Matthew 19, are but hard-rhyming necessities, brought about by the hardness of human hearts as lesser evils, as the law of Moses seeks to regulate sinful, east of Eden, human fallenness.

The permanent purposes of God in Genesis 1, then, are a regular feature in marriage rites because they are reinforced in myriad ways across the mosaic of Scripture whose central and focusing image is the eternal Lord Christ.

The *BCP* (so too the *LBW*) opens with this clear reference to blessing in Genesis 1: "*We have come together in the presence of God to witness and bless the joining together of this man and this woman in Holy Matrimony. The bond and covenant of marriage was established by God in creation.*" The "from the beginning" purpose of God, as Christ refers to it in Matthew, is the lens on which the marriage ceremony opens.

What is now frequently referred to as the second creation account goes over the same ground as Genesis 1 with more specificity. Human begetting is made possible by the stability of the heavens and the earth, and their generations: Genesis 2:4 closes account one and carefully prepares for what follows. The complementarity, the overlapping character of the accounts, is what has always been assumed in the tradition as critical to how they deliver their deepest sense. Male and female are in the image of God (1:26-27). It is not good for them to be alone, 2:18 then clarifies. A helper fit for/over against the man is found that exists nowhere else in the created realm. For the *ish*, there is the separated *ishah*, taken from him and to whom he cleaves. A man leaves his father and mother and clings to his wife and they become one flesh. Leaving father and mother does not result in being alone but in being joined and in the creating of new life. This is the life God blessed in Chapter One.

The marriage rite speaks of this second key component when it states: *The union of husband and wife in heart, body, and mind is intended by God for their mutual joy; for the help and comfort given one another in prosperity and adversity; and, when it is God's will, for the procreation of children and their nurture in the knowledge and love of the Lord.* Many biblical couples have no children. Indeed often this becomes the arena in which God's mighty and wondrous, free and untamable action can occur, as with Abraham and Sarah, Elkanah and Hannah, until culminating in Mary and the Holy Spirit. Mutual joy, help, and sexual cleaving, making possible children, is fundamental to the work of God, whether such children are forthcoming or not. That remains within the mysterious purposes of God himself, inside his ordering and oversight of creation.

The marriage rite, in accordance with the rule of faith, unites the intention of God in creation with the dominical adornment and Yes in John 2. Here is the third key component. *The bond and covenant of marriage was established by God in creation, and our Lord Jesus Christ adorned this manner of life by his presence and first miracle at a wedding in Cana of Galilee.*

The Word present at creation and in the ordering purposes of God becomes flesh and now is present at a wedding at Cana. His mother – styled by John as "woman" here and at the Cross – is a new woman/Eve.[10] She proposes ("do whatever he tells you") and he disposes ("fill the jars with water"). The water of first creation becomes by his word the wine of his abundant, blessed, present-time creational "very good." His act of new-wine creation is the completion by God through the image of God, his son, of the first creational purposes of God. Working in conjunction with the obedient woman/Eve, the obedient Adam reverses the act of the first Adam. The obedient woman/Eve ("do whatever he tells you") and the New Adam manifest the glory of God made known in him. The marriage rite uses the language of adornment to

---

10. See the fine discussion of R. Brown in his AB commentary. Protestants as well as traditional Roman Catholics both note the unusual address to Mary as 'woman' and see it as conveying this New Adam figuration (*The Gospel According to John I-XII* [AB 29; New Haven: Yale, 1970]).

capture something of the grand sacrament of John 3. Who is the man and who is the woman present at this marriage? In the rites of the church, it is the couple now standing before the selfsame work of God in Christ which the rite itself embraces and calls upon for blessing. The consistent reference to John 2 in marriage rites is the third key component.

Ephesians 5 is the next text the rite calls upon consistent with the Rule of Faith's amalgamating and according purpose. *It signifies to us the mystery of the union between Christ and his Church, and Holy Scripture commends it to be honored among all people.* Paul uses the language of mystery (*sacramentum*) when he concludes his commendation to the Christian household. Quoting Genesis 2 explicitly, he writes, "For this reason a man shall leave his father and his mother and be joined to his wife, and the two shall become one flesh. This mystery is a profound one, and I am saying it refers to Christ and his church." The sexual differentiation of man and woman, and the love that overcomes and joins them, is but a figure, a mystery, pointing to the love of God in Christ for the church of his claiming and redeeming. Here is the fourth scriptural component.

The collect of the marriage service helps us understand that it will require God's sustaining grace to bring forth the love and fidelity necessary for the solemn vows undertaken to be honored and kept. There is nothing natural or created of itself that brings about the conditions for right or lasting desire, fidelity, honor or blessing. We call upon the ever-living God, through Jesus Christ, in the power of the Holy Spirit to bless what Christ blesses as the Word of Creation made flesh, as at that signal adornment in Cana of Galilee.

O gracious and everliving God, you have created us male and female in your image: Look mercifully upon this man and this woman who come to you seeking your blessing, and assist them with your grace, that with true fidelity and steadfast love they may honor and keep the promises and vows they make; through Jesus Christ our Savior, who lives and reigns with you in the unity of the Holy Spirit, one God, for ever and ever.

As the rite proceeds, we then hear read aloud from Sacred Scripture those same texts that rule and order the rite being enacted (Genesis 1; Genesis 2; Song of Solomon; Tobit), reminding us of their norming character. Not as differing options, but as all together speaking forth the selfsame mystery. The same is true of NT and Gospel texts, and the Psalms appointed. Two Psalms (127 and 128) speak of the gift of children. Psalm 67 speaks of the blessing of God in creation. That one Psalm may be more important given the age and hopes of the couple does not mean they are not all operating according to the same rule of faith. The earth bringing forth its increase (Ps. 67) bespeaks the blessing of Day Five, and his blessing of us through this evokes Day Six's culminating purpose. "Let all the earth fear him," picks up the solemn final line of the opening address to the couple and the congregation: *Therefore marriage is not to be entered into unadvisedly or lightly, but reverently, deliberately, and in accordance with the purposes for which it was instituted by God.*

The final blessing points to the final eschatological purposes of God, which far from eliminating the creational blessing enacted for the couple, crowns and projects it.

We thank you, also, for consecrating the union of man and woman in his Name. By the power of your Holy Spirit, pour out the abundance of your blessing upon this man and this woman. Defend them from every enemy. Lead them into all peace. Let their love for each other be a seal upon their hearts, a mantle about their shoulders, and a crown upon their foreheads. Bless them in their work and in their companionship; in their sleeping and in their waking; in their joys and in their sorrows; in their life and in their death. Finally, in your mercy, bring them to that table where your saints feast for ever in your heavenly home; through Jesus Christ our Lord, who with you and the Holy Spirit lives and reigns, one God, for ever and ever. Amen.

The prayer unites the protological purpose of God in Genesis with the eschatological hope of Revelation, inside of which the joyous and gracious notes of Song of Songs give refrain.

What the Rule of Faith guards against is selection and discrete literalism, whereby texts are not brought into conjunction and seen to be mutually illuminating, but played off of one another via chronology or simple preference. The Rule allows to arise the full-orbed network of associations the texts themselves call forth, from Genesis 1 to Genesis 2 to Hosea to the Psalms to Song of Songs to Matthew 19 and John 3, Ephesians 5, Colossians 3 and right up to the close of the NT canon (Revelation).

Conclusion

To speak of ethics is to speak of the Scriptures' making their force known through the rites of the church that solemnize marriage in accordance with the logic of the rule of faith. I am providing only one example of such a rite from my own context. Thomas Cranmer's greatest accomplishment was the production of deeply scriptural rites that operate within the fullest scope of the rule of faith.

Over against this accomplishment, proponents of same-sex marriage will therefore have several choices before them.

1. They can reject the plain sense articulation of the rites as such, and try to bring in a generic version that avoids the specificity of the biblical texts. This resembles the gnostic appeal to Scripture as metaphor or a "for-instance," en route to a present improvement enlivened by appeals to higher insight.

2. They can declare the rites impossible to retain and construct altogether new ones. This is closer to the Marcionite instinct. Search about within the canvass of Scripture for

those bits that reinforce what is wanted: Jesus as engendering virtues like love and hoped-for permanence in relationships, unrelated to male and female differentiation and difference.

3. They can let either of the above options co-exist with rites such as are described above, in the between-time march for their eventual elimination.

I mention this in conclusion because these things will happen or have already begun to happen. The word "marriage" is being altered and the goal of "marriage equality" is now fully part of our confused cultural and religious landscape.

What Christians can do is explain, commend, and defend the logic of the rites presently in place; maintain these as a rule of faith best capturing the totality of the Scripture's witness, including Christ's own stated logic over the breadth of the scriptural testimony to him; and be prepared to understand the identity of the church as an increasingly minority witness to the truth as handed down from Scripture and the scriptural impress on preaching, catechesis and liturgical ethics over the ages. Others will operate with versions of scriptural witness that should be familiar to us from the life of the early church, where they represented distinct challenges. We may take it as a given that we will have to be as robust and clear about how Scripture informs the rites we are unwilling to forfeit, no matter what other options others wish to pursue, for this present season of confusion and a poverty of rightly hearing God's Word. It can surely be no bad thing, and requisite upon us, to go to school again and hear how it is that God speaks through the totality of his Word.

Especially critical will be learning how to hear the Old Testament as Christian Scripture, through the fog of developmentalism, historicism, consumerist choice, and individual preference that now blankets our churches, our culture, and our theological training centers. When Christ appeals to God's purposes in creation, he is allowing the Scriptures of Israel to rhyme with his own eternal life with God, as those Scriptures set him forth, and as the early church will proclaim when it declares his life, death and rising as in accordance with them (1 Cor. 15:3).

As one church father put it, the rule of faith is the harmony of the covenants at the coming of the Lord. That harmony one must seek through prayer and fasting to discern. Difficulty is not overcome by selection or pitting one portion against another, but by deep penetration into the Scripture's totality, where Christ lives. This is the accomplishment of the marriage rites as ethical works norming the life of those who come for his blessing, as once he adorned the marriage at Cana of Galilee.

Made in the USA
Middletown, DE
13 April 2015